THE TRAIL
OF A SPORTSMAN

By Duane Bernard

Thanks for The help John.

Duane Bernard

With a Foreword by Larry Irwin, PhD

THE TRAIL OF A SPORTSMAN

By Duane Bernard

With a Foreword by Larry Irwin, PhD.

Copyright 2005 by Duane Bernard

Published in the United States of America

Library of Congress Control Number: 2005932743

ISBN 1-931291-48-9 (softcover)
ISBN 1-931291-49-7 (hardcover)

First Edition

STONEYDALE PRESS PUBLISHING COMPANY
523 Main Street • P.O. Box 188
Stevensville, Montana 59870
Phone: 406-777-2729
Email: stoneydale@montana.com

DEDICATION

This book is dedicated to my wife, Joanne, who has always been there. I thank her and appreciate that.

ACKNOWLEDGMENTS

Several of the stories in this book were previously published in slightly different form in other outdoor publications. They include:

• Chapter 2 – The story titled "Bill's Record Book Bulls" appeared in the *Oregon Record Book*.

• Chapter 13 – The story titled "More B.C. Hunts" appeared in *Hunt* magazine.

• Chapter 14 – The story titled "Quebec Caribou Hunt (1988) appeared in *Hunt* magazine.

• Chapter 15 – The story titled "Once in a Lifetime Twice" appeared in *Petersen's Hunting* magazine.

• Chapter 22 – The story titled "Rolling Stone Rams" appeared in *Safari* magazine.

Table of Contents

Cover Photo: Author Duane Bernard and wife, Joanne, with a bighorn sheep taken in 1988.

Foreword

Probably most folks believe the old saw, "Once in a while you get lucky". I believe that good things don't just happen – they result from Divine appointment. So, it was to my eternal fortune to meet and get to know Duane Bernard and his wife, Joanne, here in Montana's Bitterroot Valley in the summer of 2001. Being the observant one, he noticed my baseball cap, upon which was embroidered the word Namibia and a gemsbok (or oryx) logo. My hat suggested that I was a hunter. It turned out that we had friends and places in common, and it wasn't long before we were swapping hunting adventures. Such is a time-honored means by which men interact, which is why you'll truly enjoy the adventures and misadventures in *"The Trail of A Sportsman"*. I'm honored to write a few words about those tales of his life as a hunter-conservationist.

Before I describe Duane's book, I first feel obliged to tell you what I've learned about Duane as a man. You learn about a man quickly by hunting with him, sharing campfires, and listening to the way he talks about his adventures. In Duane's case, there is no pretension, no brag, just fact. Clearly, he is cut from fine cloth. I've learned that he doesn't waver from the truth – ever. Neither does he stray from the proverbial road less traveled: that of a true sportsman's ethics. His ethics are not negotiable, and that steadfastness has carried over to his business dealings and other interactions. He is a family man and a man of Faith. I have yet to meet a more dedicated hunter who so ardently promotes our hunting heritage while also delighting in sharing a campfire and a cup of coffee, or discussing contemporary hunting or conservation topics. There is an old saying in Texas, ascribed only to those of the highest moral and ethical fiber: "He'll do to ride the River with". I would gladly ride the River with him, anyplace, anytime.

It is oft said, "Behind every good man stands a good woman." The same is true for Duane. Any man would be blessed with a wife who would endure with aplomb, as his wife Joanne has, the long plane rides, the cold and wet horseback rides, and the worrisome waits. In Duane's case, Joanne has been so much more for him: she has been an endearing companion who truly wanted to be with him to share fully in his adventures. A man could not wish for a finer companion than Joanne, and the book is every bit as much about her adventures and about her mettle as it is his over their nearly 50 years together.

Duane's life adventures as a hunter are perhaps not unique, but are compelling and often gripping. From starting out with a .22 rifle as most hunters do, then advancing to a .30-30, and eventually traveling on international hunts with a "7-mag" and .375 H&H, Duane spritely tells his life-long hunting tales. You can almost feel the chilling Alaskan winds biting your face, taste Joanne's steaks, or smell the fresh mountain air. Or smell the campfire coffee. In fact, knowing how he likes his coffee, I suspect that on one of his more worrisome adventures, he actually sniffed out the jar of freeze-dried coffee that he found.

Duane shares his hunting stories such that you feel invited. From Namibia to the Limpopo River in northern South Africa (where I'll be in a week), to New Zealand (where I now want to go), to Alaska, Quebec and New Mexico, Duane describes exciting adventures so riveting that you'll read the book from cover to cover. You'll feel like you've shared personally in those adventures, and, like me, you'll yearn to hike some of the same trails.

Larry D. Irwin, PhD
Stevensville, Montana
July 26, 2005

Introduction

This book came about mainly as my desire to leave some knowledge of my hunts and travels to my grandkids. I want them and others younger than me to be aware of the prices and procedures in the "old days". The hunts described in this book are by no means the only ones this sportsman took. There were hundreds more, some good and some not so good. It is also my desire to urge both young and older hunters to get out and go hunting, and not just in your home state either. If you have a desire to hunt in some other state or country, plan for it and do it. Believe me when I say that if I can do it you can. You don't have to be wealthy to go hunting, you just need to have the desire to go.

One more bit of advice I'll add here is for more hunters to get involved with the sportsmen's organizations like Safari Club International, National Rifle Association, Oregon Hunter's Association, Rocky Mountain Elk Foundation, Mule Deer Foundation, Ducks Unlimited, Foundation for North American Wild Sheep, and Pheasants Forever. Don't sit back and leave it to the others to protect your right to hunt and own a firearm. Do your share and a little more.

Duane Bernard
Rainier, Oregon
July, 2005

Author and wife, Joanne, at the Safari Club International office in Washington, D.C.

Chapter One

THE EARLY YEARS

Home to me was a small country home in rural Columbia County, Oregon, where I grew up in the 1940's and early 50's having moved there with my parents in 1939 as a toddler. The effects of the Depression were still very apparent in those early years. My folks had no money but did manage to buy 21 acres of alder and second growth fir from the county for the fair market value of $65.00. They were able to pay it off in three payments. It was land the county had foreclosed on for lack of tax payments by the original timber company owners. The county begged them to buy more, but the folks didn't think they had a need for more. Many is the time that I've regretted their short-sightedness. My father soon got a job working for the county road department. The county owned a rock pit about a quarter mile from the home he built for us so it was very convenient for him. The roads were all gravel at that time except for one or two state highways that crossed the county. Later on my father drove log truck on the road past our rural home. His was the only log truck hauling then. He made one trip in the morning and one in the afternoon, usually stopping by our house for lunch mid-day. I still live on that same road (paved now) and many times I see four to five log trucks going by our home at one time.

This area was very remote and wild then. I know, as I remember walking the two miles to school each day. That was the only way to get to the old school where about 20 to 25 kids were in the eight grades. My mother never learned to drive so she used to worry about me walking that distance as it was all open range then. Some of those old range bulls could be nasty. I clearly remember when the electric power line was installed along the road. Also, when the phone line was added to it! I remember too when the road was paved and also when it was rebuilt and straightened years later. Life was entirely different then. There were only a few cars a day by our old home and we knew who was driving each one and probably knew where they were going. There was a milk truck that came by three times a week to pick up milk and cream from the people that had any to sell. The bread truck came by once a week so we could buy bread and pastry. The Watkins man came through the area three to four times a year selling his products. My folks drove to a small store down on the Columbia River about once a week to buy groceries, gasoline and feed for our cows, pigs and chickens. The entire complex there was built on piling out over the river and while mom and dad were shopping I'd run to the edge of the dock and watch the many commercial fishermen unload their heavily loaded boats. The river, it seemed, was full of salmon at most any time of the year. This entire little town built over the river is all gone today as is that way of life. Three sisters eventually joined me to make our little family.

One thing that I still remember vividly happened on a cold snowy day. At this time I usually rode a school bus to school, but we'd been snowed in for a week or more and there was no traffic at all on the road by our house. I owned a little Stevens single shot .22 and decided to hike up through the brush about a mile to a neighbors house where two boys about my age lived. I think I was about ten at the time. I did NOT take my .22 but one of those boys owned one exactly like mine and he suggested that we take a hike out behind his house and take his .22 rifle with us and do some target practicing. Sounded good to me! When we got about a quarter of a mile from his house we commenced to shoot a few shots with him shooting first as it was his gun. It was snowing about as hard as possible. After he took a few shots he offered me the gun. I loaded the single shot and raised it up to shoot as he stood behind me. At that time I shot right-handed, but later on I switched to shooting left-handed. Anyway, when I was just about to pull the trigger, he said to wait a bit and he'd wipe the snow from the top of the barrel. As he was saying this he was also reaching up under my right elbow to grab the gun and pull it back down to wipe the snow off the barrel so I could see the sights better. Well my trigger finger was already on the trigger in the trigger guard and my left hand cradled the forearm. As he pulled the gun down and back toward him, my finger stuck in the trigger guard and on the trigger just as the end of the barrel cleared my left hand. I hollered at him to wait, but too late. The gun fired hitting two fingers on my left hand (the little one and the ring finger). It broke the ring finger. Kids with guns!!! I wrapped my handkerchief around it and we started back to his house. There was really nothing his mother could do, so she sent me on home. There were no phones there then and we were all snowed in and four-wheel drive was still unheard of so I put the hand in my pocket and walked the mile through the woods to our house. Mom wasn't able to do much for me either except make me a bed by the wood stove on the floor of the living room where it was nice and warm. That was a rough night. All we had for pain was aspirins. They helped but it sure did throb and hurt that night. Mom and I made a splint for it, but we didn't do too well and it is still very crooked and stiff today.

Another family near us also had four children and my folks were good friends with them. The Curtis family consisted of three sons and one daughter (exact opposite of ours) along with the parents, Bill and his wife, Doris. Bill was a logger and a farmer, but most of all Bill was a hunter. An outdoorsman! A real old time mountain man! Also a trapper! Bill became my mentor at an early age. Those feelings really increased at about age ten when my own father left home. Several years later my mother divorced him. I saw very little of him until my own marriage. Bill and his wife were good neighbors and helped my mother and I many times. Although Bill had three sons, none of them were as enthralled with the outdoors and hunting as their father was. But I sure was! Bill was a hunter 'til the day he died and it looks like that same situation awaits me. We became life long friends.

I used to enjoy either taking my old horse several miles into the wild brushy country behind our home to hunt or just hiking back there to better learn the area and the habits of the deer. This country was absolutely overrun with deer at that time. No elk yet but the deer numbers were unbelievable. In the early 1900's this country was logged extensively and completely. This was way before reforestation was heard of, at least locally. This logging of the land created a perfect deer habitat. Also there were few hunters, darned few roads and no four-wheel drive vehicles in public use yet. All of this made for ideal blacktail deer habitat and hunting.

It was on one of these early hunts in October of 1952 behind our house where I got my very first blacktail buck. I had left home very early to hike back in to an area that was usually good for seeing many deer. I was carrying an old beat up .30-30 Winchester model '94 that my dad had left behind. I had learned to shoot entirely on my own and had absolutely no idea of the limitations of that old .30-30. I soon spotted a buck across the large (very large) canyon and commenced firing. After more shots than that old buck had probably heard in his entire life he finally showed sign of being mortally wounded. I'd been so far away that I don't think he even knew that he was being shot at. He suddenly took off running straight down the very steep hill that he'd been standing on apparently enjoying that beautiful October morning. I put the gun on "safe" and started running down my side of the canyon where I had to cross the good sized creek that ran year 'round there. To my dismay I could not find him. I walked up the steep hill to where he had been when I shot. I found some deer hair, but no deer blood. Only big tracks about 20 feet apart where he had bounded down the mountain. Talk about being discouraged! I went down to the creek again and walked up and down it looking very closely for his tracks or blood. Being so young and inexperienced and without any adult help I was unable to locate the buck. At that young age I never thought to look across the creek. I did not know they would cross water like that.

I returned home via the Curtis ranch and told Bill my sad story. He knew the area well and knew exactly where this all happened. Several days later Bill went in there to have a look and of course he had no trouble locating a very large and smelly blacktail buck on the opposite side of the creek from where I'd looked so hard. Shows what experience can add to a hunt, but experience only comes with time. Bill cut the horns off and brought them out to his place. The next time I saw him he offered them to me but I rejected his offer as I was so disgusted with myself because I'd failed to find the buck myself. It was many, many years later before I finally listened to him and took them home. I cleaned them up, measured them, bought a cape for them and had the old buck mounted at last. He made the B&C record book with a score of 133 5/8. My first buck!

While in high school I met a young lady in my class that I enjoyed spending time with by the name of Joanne Bentley. She liked to fish in the Columbia River and she really liked to ride around the local hills in my old '42 Willy's Jeep which I had bought while in high school. I taught her how to shoot a rifle and later on her dad would join us on deer hunts. Well, I guess I still enjoy spending time with her as we approach the golden anniversary before too long. She doesn't hunt any more, but still goes with me on nearly all trips. We've traveled a good share of this old world together and she has hunted a lot of it too. When in the early days of our lives I introduced her to Bill Curtis, she took an immediate liking to him also

Bill Curtis with his two record book bulls.

Chapter Two

BILL'S RECORD BOOK BULLS

A great many hunters pursue the majestic elk. Some of them kill bulls. A few consistently kill bulls. Very few kill record book bulls and the number of hunters putting more than one bull in the record book is minuscule at best. Bill Curtis was of that rare breed. He passed away when I was fifty years old and up until that time we were not only neighbors, but close friends and hunting partners. I submit this chapter in this book to give you, the reader, a better understanding of my background and of my mentoring with Bill in my youth.

During my childhood there were no elk within about 30 miles of our northwest Oregon home, so you can imagine my surprise when I stumbled on a lone set of huge elk tracks in the vicinity of our house. Of course when I mentioned my find to Bill, he was already aware of the gigantic Roosevelt roaming in our midst. We had seen these tracks and rubs in deer season but it was quite a few years before I was to see my first live elk.

Bill decided he would hunt this bull, this newcomer to our area. His hunts didn't require much planning or preparation as he usually hunted quite near home, possibly due to finances. No big deal – just "go out and fetch some meat". The planning consisted of deciding which trails to take to get there. As for the preparation, just grab the old .30-30 Winchester, model # 94, put on his hat and coat and possibly catch and saddle his horse. Then he'd slip off out through the large alder trees and the towering firs on one of the many horse trails he'd cut through the vine maples to some of his favorite "fern patches".

Well he spent several days hunting that big bull elk before he found tracks fresh enough to work. Bill then tied up the saddle horse, slipped his old .30-30 out of the black homemade scabbard and got real serious about this business of "fetchin' some meat". He followed that bull until nearly dark and then merely backtracked to his horse, built a small fire and munched on some of his homemade jerky and apples. It wasn't a very comfortable night but at least it didn't rain. Notice that I didn't mention a sleeping bag or tent or Coleman stove and lantern.

Come first light the next morning Bill was on the bull's tracks. He finally got his chance and had slipped in real close to the bull when it finally jumped out of its bed and was in the middle of its last bound when Bill levered several shots into his huge body. He was elated when he walked up to his big bull. He knew it was a big one, but the 9x7 rack surprised even Bill. Years later when measured it scored 322 3/8 B & C and 356 6/8 SCI. This easily placed it in both record books.

He had a heck of a time butchering this large animal. The carcass was cut into nine chunks because he was unable to lift the quarters. Back at his house and before he hung it up in his large pump house the nine pieces weighed 735 pounds. If you mentally add on the liver, heart, head, antlers, and lower legs you begin to get an idea of the size of this trophy.

No fanfare, no pictures, no driving around town with the head on the front bumper and no calls to the taxidermist. (Bill would put the horns on a board at a later date.) He had merely gone out and "fetched some meat".

A few years later he commenced to see another huge set of elk tracks in the same area. He put the same old .30-30 in the same old black homemade leather saddle boot and rode out. He got lucky! As he rode into the area where the big bull had been living , he spotted the huge bull up ahead of him with its head and antlers up in a tall elderberry bush. It was breaking off the branches with its massive horns and eating them. This is very common for bulls to do after the rut when they're trying to regain the weight they lost in the rutting season. The bull was totally oblivious to Bill's presence. At the shot (about 75 yards) the big bull just wheeled and ran off. When Bill got up there he couldn't find a trace of blood, hair or the elk. Nothing! He followed that bull the rest of the weekend without seeing it again. It was obviously not hurt as Bill didn't find one drop of blood and Bill didn't usually miss. Frustrated and tired he returned home Sunday night and prepared for work as usual Monday morning. All week long this gnawed at him. How could he have missed? Maybe he should have aimed for the lungs instead of the head, he kept thinking to himself. But why wasn't there at least some blood or hair?

That was one long week for Bill but the next weekend finally rolled around and Bill was again back on the ridge determined to find the big bull. It didn't take him long to find the tracks and he was able to follow them right up to the bull. When it started to jump and run, Bill fired three very quick shots with the lever action right into the lungs from only a few yards away. He now had his second trophy bull elk, a huge 6x6 that years later scored 315 4/8 B&C and 331 6/8 SCI. Not bad, I'd say! Bill killed the first bull in November of 1952 and the second one in November of 1965.

This bull was not fat and round like the first one had been. It was very skinny. Its paunch was empty and later on we'd find out that the meat was very tough.

After butchering the elk and before he cut off the horns, Bill began to remove the "elk ivory" – "the whistlers". SURPRISE!!! The bull only had one whistler. The spot in the jaw where the other ivory had been was nearly healed from the damage that Bill's .30-30 bullet had inflicted a week earlier. Now it all made sense. It all came together. That's why the bull was so skinny and his paunch was empty. Now Bill knew why there had been no blood a week earlier. Bill had shot for the head as the bull had his head up in the brush eating and when hit the bull had merely closed his mouth and ran off. The eyeguard still shows today where the bullet nicked it after taking out the whistler tooth. This should also explain to all why Bill's old .30-30 had an odd number of elk teeth in the stock.

How many hunters do you know who have put two bull elk in the B&C record book, hunting alone and unguided? How many could go back a week later pick up the track, follow it up and then kill the same bull? I'll admit that there were practically no other hunters hunting elk here then. Also there were almost no elk here then, just the odd old bull that had strayed in. This did work in Bill's favor but still Bill was of a rare breed and I feel fortunate to have known him, hunted with him, and been his neighbor for so many years. I'm certain that he inspired me to go on and do the extensive hunting and traveling that I've done for many different species in several different countries.

I always admired those two big sets of elk horns and if I had company from out of town I'd often take them to Bill's house so they could see them and meet the hunter who killed them. Bill knew that I cherished those horns more than anyone except he, himself. I guess that is the reason that he willed them to me. I still cherish them.

Some have mixed feelings about displaying trophies in their den or office that they themselves didn't shoot. Well, I feel honored to have two big sets of Boone and Crockett elk horns on my wall that my dear friend killed and later willed to me. One even has that little knick in the eyeguard where a .30-30 bullet scraped across it from an old model '94 Winchester fired by an old-timer many years ago. Thanks Bill.........

Chapter Three

BRITISH COLUMBIA MOOSE HUNT

Like so many others, I wanted to go to British Columbia on a moose hunt. I thought we could possibly afford it if I could find the right hunt. I wanted Joanne to go along too. I'd met some outfitters from there and had heard of a few more that weren't too expensive. You gotta start somewhere, so I started by writing a few inquiries. My first letter was to Mr. Eric Collier of Riske Creek, B.C. He had written a very interesting book which I still own, called *"Three Against The Wilderness"*. Mr. Collier had done some guiding but was not involved at that time (this was 1962).

I'd been keeping an ear to the ground regarding moose guides so in early 1970 when I inquired about a hunt with a Mr. Hiram Cutler of Prince George, B.C., and he returned a note saying he had room for us that fall I got real interested. His references checked out, we could afford the $175.00 per hunter that he wanted and he said that we'd hunt black bear and moose. I asked my father-in-law, Onie, if he'd like to join us. He was recently retired but he realized the opportunity here and thought he could afford the price.

Hiram lived with his wife and two daughters 67 miles southwest of Prince George. He owned a ranch there in that beautiful, remote mountain country. Jo and I would share one log cabin and Onie would have another to himself. This wasn't to be a fancy hunt or a trophy hunt, but just a meat hunt for a bull moose and possibly a bear. We sent him our $75.00 deposits. We booked the hunt, and was Onie ever excited! I suppose Jo and I were too, but not like he was. When we returned from that hunt we went over to eastern Oregon a few days later and Onie was still telling anyone who'd listen about his moose hunt. For the money we had quite a hunt. Onie and I teamed up on a small bull moose. The first one for either of us! Then I shot a yearling black bear cub, my first. The experience was great, we got along fine, we saw game and even brought some meat home. What more could we expect for $175.00?

Our moose camp in British Columbia in 1970.

After the hunt we checked the meat in a cooler in Quesnel, B.C., and looked up a friend we knew in that very neat little town. His name was Ross Rollins and he was quite the singer and entertainer. He also liked to fish, camp and hunt. We suggested a few days fishing and grouse hunting out on the Nazco River and he was all for it. Good ol' Ross, he was always fun to be with. The fishing was good, the company and the scenery were the best and I've never seen grouse hunting like that before or since. We were there four to five days and then started south towards home. I knew then that I could get hooked on this big game hunting away from home.

Packing out our first ever moose.

Chapter Four

ELK HUNTING IN HELL'S CANYON

It was in the fall of 1969 when I put together an elk hunting trip to Hell's Canyon on the Oregon-Idaho border for Onie (Joanne's dad), Delmer (a good friend of mine) and myself. I had a saddle horse but did not have the equipment on knowledge to go in there without professional help so I called a fellow I'd heard of that lived and guided in that area and made arrangements for him to pack us in on the day before elk season. The guide's name was Jack Hooker. He had came to Oregon from Montana and a few years later after he lost his wife here, he returned to Montana. I still occasionally bump into him at RMEF or SCI conventions.

Onie was not a horseman. Period!

Delmer and I had hunted together quite a lot and got along fine, regardless of the fact that he was totally deaf and unable to speak at all. He'd taught me sign language years before so communication wasn't a problem. I must say here and now, although Delmer has been dead for years, he was one of the best hunters I've ever had the pleasure to hunt with. The senses that he did possess were put to very good use. He was also an excellent bowhunter. He would target practice with his bow by having someone bounce a soft rubber ball across the yard and he hit that ball more than he missed. Try it sometime.

Prior to Oregon's first elk season of the year Onie, Delmer and I got together and drove to Imnaha in far eastern Oregon. We found Jack Hooker's ranch and because he had so many hunters there to be packed in the next day we were offered the chance to spread our sleeping bags out on the hay in his barn. There was no more room in his home and motels are non-existent here. Next morning (the day before the opening) we were escorted by Jack, himself down the very rugged hills and bluffs to Saddle Creek in Hells Canyon. We followed Saddle Creek aways and then Jack reined up and declared that this was a good place to camp as there was a good spring only about 100 yards away. We unloaded the mules and as soon as Jack left we started setting up our tent. However, it didn't look like we'd need it as the weather was quite warm and sunny, not good elk hunting weather at all. We scouted around camp some but there really wasn't much time that day. We'd have to do most of our scouting after the season opened in the morning.

Author on left and Delmer to the right in front of our Hell's Canyon camp.

Jack had warned us of all the bears in the area by telling us not to leave any elk out overnight if and when we killed one. He also said to keep our groceries put up where the bears couldn't reach them or we'd end up having trouble. Wanting to get an early start the next morning, we went to bed early and because it was so warm out, we left the flaps open and tied back out of the way on the 9x12 wall tent. Our groceries had been suspended from a rope we had strung between two trees. Delmer had found some old tin cans and placed a few pebbles in them and them tied them to a string and hung them below the grocery bags. This should alert us (not him) to any bears messing with our grub. We blew out the lantern and crawled in the bags. Before any of us were asleep Onie and I could hear something rustling around near the tent. We heard twigs snapping. Next we heard something stepping on some plastic visqueen that we had packed in to protect our gear from rain or snow. Then something brushed against one of the tent ropes. That did it. It was time to investigate. Meanwhile, of course Delmer couldn't hear any of this, but he knew that Onie and I were concerned about something. When I tried to get out of my sleeping bag quietly to have a look-see around we heard a commotion outside the tent as something quite large was leaving very fast. I grabbed a flashlight and my rifle, which is always near me, and hurried out to look around. No bear in sight! But he'd been there and when he left in a hurry he knocked over our newly opened three-pound can of coffee. That made him enemy # 1 in my book. I like my coffee. Ever try to sort coffee grounds from pine needles? Ever try to drink coffee made with a few pine needles in it?

Back to bed and to sleep this time, but the war was on. Quiet the rest of the night but it took awhile to get Delmer quieted down. He was very surprised to find out that the bear had been within six to seven feet of us lying there on our air mattresses on the ground.

At dawn we went our separate ways but none of us felt like we wanted to leave camp too far while that bear was still around, so we each came back in throughout the day to check on camp. Once when I returned I found our plastic water bucket was on the ground with tooth marks in it. Not good when you need it to carry water 100 yards from the spring. The bear had also gotten into some bread dough that Joanne had prepared for us to take along. I love to fry it in a skillet and put butter and/or jam on it. Stolen bread dough, spilled coffee grounds and a leaking water bucket; that bear had to go! There were no elk close by anyway. Too warm and the elk were way up higher. None of us had seen any elk close by, although while glassing for elk Delmer had seen a cougar way off.

That night we would do things a bit differently, as we expected the bear to return. We made sure the tent flaps were tied back, rifles loaded and right by us and we'd built a fire in a strategically perfect area to aid our efforts in dispatching the bear. The fire was about 30 feet out in front of our open tent and lit up the whole area quite well. We started letting it die down well before we were ready to go to bed so that hopefully we'd not have too long to wait.

Not to disappoint us, the bear showed up in ten to fifteen minutes after we went to bed. We first heard some twigs breaking behind the tent, then a few minutes later he was over beside the tent although we couldn't see him yet. All this time Delmer was so excited. He knew we were hearing the bear, but he didn't know where the bear was or how close he was. Imagine our surprise when the bear walked UNDER the tent rope, right within five to six feet of our feet and so well outlined as he was between us and the fire. Thankfully, my rifle was loaded and on my lap. We were already sitting up in bed. I only had to raise the rifle and push the safety off and I was ready to pull the trigger and end our bear problems (I hoped). You can't imagine the size a black bear appears to be when you're looking up at him from a sleeping bag. We found him the next morning about 100 yards away and very dead. His hide is about fifteen feet from me as I write this.

We never saw any bulls. The weather was just too nice, but we never had any more bear trouble either. Jack came in at the requested time and we began the long upward journey out of the deepest canyon in North America, beautiful Hell's Canyon.

Delmer and Onie with the bear hide in the foreground.

Chapter Five

A TOUGH NIGHT IN HELL'S CANYON

As near as I can remember it was October of '72 before I went back to Hell's Canyon. This time I was deer hunting in October. I'd asked a neighbor of ours (Bob) if he'd like to join me. I would be taking my twin boys along although they were s bit too young to hunt yet, so I asked him to bring his son of about the same age as company for Dave and Dan, my sons.

We took two rigs, a four-wheel drive, three-quarter- ton pickup with a winch and a CJ 5 Jeep with a winch. Leaving civilization at Imnaha, Oregon, we headed up towards Hat Point. From there we planned on following the old road that runs north along the top of the ridge for several miles out to the general area I wanted to hunt . This was the first time out that way for all of us. I'd not hunted there before, but had heard some good reports of that area.

We were able to find the old "jeep" road that runs for miles out that ridge and managed to follow it pretty well, stopping only occasionally to cut a tree out of the way. That evening we pitched the tents and set up a swell camp and had time to do a little glassing too from right near camp. Everywhere you look from here is down, there is no such thing as up, just down. The Snake River is over a mile below you in the bottom of the gigantic canyon. We were camped at about 7,000 feet elevation. Remember that!

The next day Bob and I each took our sons and headed out to see if we could locate any bucks. This is extremely rough and rugged country and it's just not a country that you do a lot of walking in. Best to stop and glass and then stalk if need be. There are many small bluffs from eight to twenty feet high. It is mountain goat country and sheep too as well as mule deer. Bob and I both arrived back at camp about the same time.

Our deer camp on the rim of Hell's Canyon, before it snowed.

Around 10:30 or so I think. We fixed a big breakfast and hung around camp 'til about 3:30 or 4:00 and then we set out to see if we could spot a buck before dark. The boys had seen enough of that steep canyon for one day, so they wanted to stay in camp and wait for us. They were old enough to be careful and to behave without us being there. Kinda that awkward age, old enough to want to go along, but not old enough to legally carry a rifle.

Bob and I told them we wouldn't be gone too long and that we just intended to drop down below camp a ways and sit to glass. We'd probably be within 400 yards of them at all times. We built them a big rip-roaring fire and got some extra wood up for them. The weather was nice; just a real nice fall day. Warm and sunny!

We left camp and walked only a short way to a good viewpoint to set and glass. We remained together and whispered back and forth to each other as we watched for deer. It wasn't too long before we spotted a decent buck, nothing huge, but he'd do, so we flipped a coin to see who'd take the shot. He was quite a way below us and had no idea there was anyone around so we had plenty of time. Bob won the coin toss. He shot and hit the buck, but the deer didn't go down. Bob's second shot as the deer was trying to run away missed completely. Well we had shot, so we had to go look for blood. That's the rule in our camp. The last time I saw the buck he was going back to our left toward the area he had came from. We managed to get down to the place he'd been in when Bob shot and found a little blood and hair from him, but no buck. There were so many boulders here that we could not find his tracks to follow them, but would find a drop or two of blood once in awhile. When it was almost dark and we knew we'd have to quit and give up for that day we could no longer see camp above us, but both knew we were directly below camp. We had came down into the canyon south of our camp, then Bob shot and we trailed the buck north aways and so when we had to quit we decided to just take the shortest route back to our tent, which was right straight up the hill. We started up and it was like climbing a giant set of stairs with each step being three to four feet high. Before too long the step size increased to about four to five feet high, but it was now dark enough that we could see the fire in front of the tent. The boys had built it up to a pretty good size when we didn't show up when they figured we should. It really wasn't all that far away. All we had to do we thought was continue uphill (west). It was getting dark fast now as the sun was down, but we were heading up into that bright western sunset so could still see pretty good. Soon the steps got even higher and we had to help each other over them, which took longer. About this time we noticed the ridge we had been following up out of the canyon had been getting narrow (extremely narrow). It was only about five to six feet wide now and we would have been able to walk it and look down both sides at once if it had been daylight. But it wasn't daylight and it was getting very scary. It was too dark to see how far down it was to the ground but I found an egg-sized rock and threw it over the side. WOW! It was a long way down. Another small rock confirmed the same thing with the other side. Now we also became aware of the fact that we could still see somewhat when looking west (up toward camp), but could see absolutely nothing if we tried looking back down the way we'd come. We knew we had to be extremely careful here without a flashlight, but took solace in the fact that we didn't have much further to go. After crawling on hands and knees for about 50 feet on top of this "rock wall" we encountered another of those steps, up about five feet and then a flat spot about the size of a double bed which was backed up next to another BIG step up. It looked about ten to twelve feet straight up and there was no way on earth we could get over it. When we turned to look back down the way we'd came up we could not see a thing, nor could we now see the camp fire, but the western sky was still rather bright.

Bob was wearing a heavy down coat and no cap or hat. I was wearing a good warm cap but no coat. We both wore Levis and no gloves. We had matches but what to burn on a solid rock slab? I'd not taken a coat because we weren't going far and it had been a nice warm day, remember? Also remember that I said this is about 7,000 feet elevation, in OCTOBER. There was only one choice and we didn't like it. It would have been very foolish to try to get back down without a flashlight. I'll tell you that the term "warm weather" or warm night is only relative. It was a hell of a long way from warm on that mountain that night. Because I had no coat and Bob did have one I lay down next to the rock face and he layed right up next to me but more exposed to the wind. Not a strong wind, thank God, but a wind never the less! When we got too cold or too stiff we both would turn over the other way. We stayed cuddled close together. When we got too cold one of us would get up on his knees and hold on to the other's belt while the one standing done a little jig to try and get the circulation going again. We'd wave the arms at the same time as best we could to warm up some, then we'd trade places and the other one would try to warm up the same way. You had to have the other one hold on to you or you couldn't stay on the small flat surface and we knew it was a long way down. It was hard to stand at first. It was also quite hard to talk. We were getting very hypothermic. It was a clear night, which meant no snow. We hardly slept at all. The later it got the colder we got. We were also getting stiffer all the time and by the first hint of daylight we were ready to start down but were so cold we could barely navigate, especially down over those steps and believe me we CRAWLED along the top of that rock wall, which was flat and about two feet wide on the average.

After a half hour or so we began to warm up a little but our joints still ached and we still had trouble talking. We had been very, very cold. When we finally got to the bottom we could then move faster and we felt safe then so we hurried over to where we had came down the afternoon before. From there we walked back up the hill and it actually felt good because we were warming up.

We got to camp just as the boys were getting up and it was a very happy reunion. We fixed a BIG breakfast.

That night it snowed. Only a couple of inches, but had it of came one night sooner, I doubt very much if I'd be here today. I've never been that cold and don't want to go through it again.

The following day I killed a buck and we were able to winch him out with the Jeep. Then we packed up and headed out of there while we could. Get while the getting's good!. We had to winch the pickup up over one little hill and had to be careful due to the snow but we were darned glad to be able to leave there. I've never been back and I've never been that cold since.

Warning sign at the start of the new Cassier Highway, the 502-mile shortcut.

Chapter Six

OUR DRIVE TO ALASKA

I had always had a strong hankering to go to Alaska and my wife Joanne shared those feelings with me. On August 23, 1973. we lined up a babysitter for our four kids and loaded up our '67 four-wheel drive pickup and started out for the north country. I had arranged five weeks vacation. We allowed one week traveling each way and that would leave us three weeks to hunt, fish, look around or whatever. We had an eight foot camper on the three-quarter-ton truck and pulled a small, but very strong utility trailer with what would in later years become known as an ATV in it. The ATV was a two-wheel drive motorcycle made by Rokon Industries. They're still made today but not nearly as popular as the four-wheeled imported models. We had a detachable side car for ours. Joanne would ride behind me and we'd carry our lunch, packs, game etc. in the small side car. It was rather slow (like a tractor) but would go almost anywhere you had enough nerve to take it. I once rode it over a picnic table with ease, but that's not to be mentioned here.

We left home in early September and drove to British Columbia, Canada. The border crossing had me very nervous as I intended to take a handgun across Canada to Alaska. I'd been told you could do it, if you told them up front about your intentions, which I did. But I was still afraid they might deny me the privilege. We breezed right through, but they did make me put the .44 magnum in a plastic bag which they sealed and then the border guard told me that it had better still be sealed when I left the Yukon to enter Alaska. It was!

We stopped in Prince George, British Columbia, the first night to spend some time with a couple that we'd known for years. Had a great time with them and even spent an extra day on their large farm. Their home was made of logs as was their barn, the tractor shed, the pump house, chicken house and all the rest of the buildings. They were quite remote and logs were plentiful while lumber was expensive I guess. While we were there they happened to mention to us that an alternate route to Alaska was being built. In fact, Owen told me that the construction crew had only the week before "pioneered" the road clear through from Watson Lake on the north end to Kitwanga on the southern end. For the uninformed, the term "pioneer" is used in road building circles to describe the very first time a large "cat" or earthmover has finally made it through the virgin area. Well, Joanne and I being of the adventuresome type decided that we were in no particular hurry. After all, we had four-wheel drive, our own camper on board, a winch on the front and three gas tanks. So what's the problem? We may as well see some new country. After all, the shortcut was only 502 miles long. This route would later on become known as the "Cassiar Highway" or highway #37.

There was a large 4'x 8' sign at the southern end of the new road warning drivers of the dangers. It read: Caution thru traffic: Do not travel unless confirmation obtained from Department of Highways at Hazelton that road is open. Extra tires, winter apparel, fuel, sleeping bags and several days supply of food essential.

The Canadian government had actually started building this road several years before when they started at Watson Lake on the north end. Hence the northernmost portion was actually paved (narrow, but paved), then the large middle portion was graveled and quite good. Further south towards where we were to start it turned into just a dirt logging road which we were very used to, but the final southern part was only pioneered through and was very rough. Where they had turned the cats around in the road it would leave a berm that was quite high so I had to go to low gear and just crawl over it in order not to spill everything from the cupboards. Along with that type nuisance was the fact that they either had no bridges there yet or they hadn't finished them yet. To say it was slow going would be an understatement. But it was an experience and a beautiful one. We saw old Indian cemeteries with the little "spirit houses" on top of them. We saw game, especially bears as the salmon were spawning in the streams. We saw wild and virgin country that few would ever see and we'd not have the chance again. We saw the gas gauge slowly go from full to half full. One thing that we didn't see, at least at the south portion, and that was traffic. Although the further north we went, the more we encountered, along with the improved roads. In this remote country if there was a need for an airstrip they merely widened a long straight stretch of the road to accommodate the small planes by tripling the width. We saw several of these. Although we had three gas tanks on board, I was not about to pass up an opportunity to buy any fuel as we'd been warned that there was none for the entire 502 miles. The mileage on our trip was not impressive anyway, but when you're driving in second and third gear most of the time, it goes fast. So when we came upon an Indian fish camp at Eddontenajon I stopped to talk to the Indians and of course inquired about any available gas. I think they sold us ten gallons. They didn't really want to spare much of it and at 85 cents a gallon I didn't want to buy much of it. These Indians had been coming here to fish for probably centuries and now the white man had built a good road right by their fish camp. Progress I guess! Now I knew we'd be able to get to the Alaska highway, or as it used to be called, the Alcan highway. We had enough gas.

One evening on this shortcut we were about ready to stop for the night when we passed an old ranch that sat not too far back off the road. There were several horses grazing in the yard and many old moose and caribou horns decorating the sheds and fence posts. This place, like the Indian's fish camp had obviously been established here for a long time before the road came by it. We pulled off the road just past here and Jo cooked supper while I relaxed and looked at the map to try to see how far we had yet to go to reach civilization. After another good supper and several cups of coffee, we decided to turn around and go back to that old ranch for a visit. Anybody living way out there had to be receptive to guests. He was! His name was Lynch Callison and he lived there alone most of the time. He was a guide in the fall, a trapper in the winter and a very interesting and nice fellow. We enjoyed our visit and I'm sure he did too. Now I'm going to skip ahead about 25 years to a Rocky Mountain Elk Foundation annual convention in Salt Lake City where Joanne and I were strolling through the exhibit hall when I happened to notice the sign on the front of this certain outfitters booth. It read "Callison Outfitters". When I got near the booth I saw moose and caribou pictures and when I spoke to him the man in the booth had a definite Canadian accent, but he was not nearly old enough to be the Lynch Callison that I'd met so many years before. I asked if he knew of a man named Lynch Callison and he proudly said that he was Lynch's son. Small world, eh? I told him the story of meeting his dad and asked him to tell his dad hello. Good, friendly, hard working, God fearing

Canadians! Never met one I didn't like.

We really enjoyed the beautiful Cassiar Mountains during the next day or so. We came upon another home that day that had a sign out in front telling any travelers that they were selling homemade gold and jade jewelry. It was time for a stop anyway. It was also, I believe, the first house we'd seen since leaving the Callison ranch the evening before. When we stepped up on the porch of the house we were met by a middle-aged woman that said she was the "jeweler" and her husband did the mining for both the gold and the jade. In fact he was out in the mine at that time. This is how they chose to scratch out a living in those remote mountains. We looked over several pieces and I finally picked one that Jo and I both liked and bought it. Joanne still has it and wears it occasionally. It is a gold maple leaf on a piece of jade, all hand mined and hand made.

Where we hit the Alaska Highway.

I believe it was the next day that we finally got to the Alaska highway. There were no businesses there at the intersection at that time, only a lonesome sign informing us which way to turn to get to Dawson Creek or Whitehorse. We chose Whitehorse, of course. When we got to Whitehorse, Yukon Territory, we stopped and spent the night. We also went through their nice museum there and took pictures of the big stern wheeler that was docked there. Lots of good old northern history in that town.

We proceeded on to the Alaska border where I had to show the fellow on the Canadian side of the border that my handgun was still sealed in the plastic bag. Coming back home a few weeks later we had to have it re-sealed there again. We went on to Tok Junction where we stopped for awhile to buy hunting licenses, tags, gas and a few groceries before turning south towards Gulkana on the Tok cut-off. At Gulkana we turned back north and drove to Paxton where we headed west on the "Denali highway", which was all gravel. We had in mind to park somewhere in the vicinity of the great Susitna River and possibly try our luck at hunting there. At that time this general area had the reputation of being a very good game country with lots of moose, caribou and bears. On August 30th on the Denali Highway we crossed over the highest pass in Alaska that you can drive over. And it was snowing! Soon the pickup started acting up and as it was getting dark and we were tired we chose to pull over and spend the night. Next morning in the daylight (and cold) I was able to determine that our fuel pump had failed us. We did not have a spare either. We were able to coast for 14 miles to the Susitna Valley and then a good samaritan towed us the remaining few miles to the Susitna Lodge where we at least had some company and a chance at getting help. The Lodge was located just a mile or so from the Susitna River so we had made it into the general area that we'd set out to hunt anyway. It could have been worse.

The first order of business of course was to try to locate a fuel pump. No easy task I soon found out. It would have to be flown out from Anchorage, if and when we could reach Anchorage by radio-phone to order one. I was told the radio-phone was very undependable here and we'd have the best chance in the evening hours. No problem, we'd just wait 'til evening and call. Well, we did get through to someone in Anchorage that night and I did tell them what I needed and where we were stranded at, but before the lady I was talking to could confirm my needs and location we were cut off and unable to re-connect. So much for that! Had she heard me or not? Did she get all the info right? The next night I tried again and was able to reach another lady somewhere between us and Anchorage. I told her what I needed and where we were at. She repeated it all to me so I knew she had it right, but of course she had no idea when I could possibly expect a plane to be coming our way. The people at the lodge told us it should only be a few days. As it turned out both parties received my request and both were able to order a fuel pump from Anchorage. The first one showed up in a couple of days when a small plane landed at the lodge. I installed the new pump and it worked fine. The next day another plane set down with another fuel pump. We had a spare now. Thank God for the bush communications even if they're not the best.

While stranded at this lodge we made friends with one of the bush pilots that was continually flying hunters into and out of the lodge. He'd fly a party out for moose and/or caribou for a few days then go back later to check on them and bring in any meat and horns they may have gotten. There were several pilots doing this while we were there but we became acquainted with only one. That was Wally Rochester from Clear, Alaska, and originally from western Washington. We had a lot in common and became good friends. We did not fly out with him to hunt from there but we sure did a lot of hunting with him over the rest of his remaining years. When we were at Susitna Lodge it was still legal to fly and hunt on the same day so some of these hunting parties were only out hunting a couple of days. I hunted around there a couple of days, taking Joanne with me on the Trailbreaker. We saw no moose but did see two large grizzlies eating a dead moose quite a way from us. Believe me, I was real glad they were a long way off because they looked to me to about the same size and shape as a Volkswagon "Beetle". That old trail breaker was good in most of that country but it was very slow. One day we heard a strange noise while out hunting and had a hard time trying to determine what it was. It seemed to be coming closer all the time. It would almost constantly squeal. When it finally rounded the bend in the trail it turned out to be a four-wheel drive Dodge pickup on tracks. They told us that they'd taken the wheels and tires off when they left the gravel highway and put on the tracks to enable them to get back in to good moose country. The ground we were on was very hard and the power steering pump in that Dodge was working very hard and squealing at every slight turn of the steering wheel. I'm sure it worked great in the muskeg though.

I have always been a big fan of Russell Annabel and I'd read that he lived at least part of the year in a little village in Alaska called Denali. We were only about two to three miles from where the road to Denali left the Denali Highway. The road (like a jeep road) into Denali was closed to the use of "motorized" vehicles if they were used as hunting vehicles. So this meant we could not take our Trailbreaker in there with a rifle too. I did very much want to meet Russell Annabel so Jo and I elected to take a rifle and just hunt our way in as we walked the six miles each way. Of course we had our lunch and some water. Upon arriving at the little settlement we, of course, did not know which cabin was his so we asked one of the few men we saw there. This village was made up of about six to eight cabins as I remember it. The fellow told us he was quite sure that Russell was not there now, as he'd been gone for several months. We walked a half a mile or so back before stopping to eat our lunch and then went back to the Denali Highway where we had parked our camper and pickup. We were both very tired that night.

The next day when we saw Wally Rochester again he said he was taking a couple of days off and would be going up to his home in Clear. He asked Jo and I if we wanted to follow him and meet his wife and spend a day in that area. We could camp in his yard. We were going no place in particular and this sounded like no place in particular so we went. When we got to the west end of the Denali Highway we turned north and had only gone a short way when we encountered a lot of heavy road construction. They were building the highway between Anchorage and Fairbanks. The highway had extended from Anchorage to Mt. McKinley National Park and from Fairbanks down past Ferry but did not connect as it does now. Now this is a major route with a lot of traffic.

We spent two days and a night at Wally's and while there met two of his guides. Wally and these fellows were quite well known locally as very good guides. He had told us of Myron and Les and now we had a chance to meet them. Les Mortenson and Myron Stokes and his wife, Mary, have been good friends since that first meeting in '73. We continue to see Les several times a year and he and I and another guy who flew for Wally by the name of Bert even teamed up on an elk hunt in New Mexico once. Les has since came down for all our kid's weddings and we've remained friends for years. All because Joanne and I took the initiative to drive to Alaska! As you'll see later on, we returned to hunt that north country several times, but that was the only time we drove up (so far). While at Wally's that time we also got to meet his camp cook, a retired navy man that went by the name of Porky! We always enjoyed Porky. He could be very comical and a lot of fun.

We went back to the Susitna area where we decided to rent an airboat and go further up the Susitna River towards the glacier to camp a few days and hopefully the hunting would be better. That airboat ride was great, the scenery some of the best in the world, but the hunting was harder than we'd been prepared for and Joanne did not like the remoteness. One very frosty morning when I went down to the river to get some water there was a large grizzly track in the frost between our little white tent and the river's edge. That pretty much did it for Jo; she

The airboat we used to get to the head of the Susitna River.

Our moose camp at the confluence of the Susitna River and Boulder Creek.

started missing the kids all of a sudden. After four or five days there we returned to the Denali Highway and our camper. We hunted several other spots and saw a few cow moose, but no bulls and we never did see a caribou. We only saw the two big grizzlies, but that was enough. All in all it had been a wonderful experience and we'd seen some beautiful mountains and met some people that would remain friends forever. It was time to start our journey south if we were to maintain the leisurely pace and still get home in the allotted time.

We headed down the long road south, but had no intention of driving the "Cassiar" route again. We took the old traditional way through Dawson Creek and the famous milepost #1. When we got to the southern portion of B.C. we decided to head a little out of our way at Cache Creek by going east there to Kamloops and then south again to Osoyoos where we crossed the border. From there we followed the Okanogan River south to Omak, Washington. Before we'd left home in August I'd read in the paper that the North Cascades Highway was to be completed and opened in September. So what an opportunity to see some more new country! We drove west 'til we crossed the summit of the Cascade mountains and because it was dark and raining very hard, we camped there along the Skagit River. Joanne had replenished our grocery supplies in Omak, including some fresh vegetables that had been scarce in our camp and that night along the beautiful wild Skagit River she outdone herself as it poured rain outside. What I feast we had! We went to bed knowing that we'd be home the next night.

We had driven 4,626 miles total and approximately 2,700 were on gravel roads, causing us five flat tires. We paid $270.00 for non-resident licenses and tags. We spent $319. 00 on gas, with the average price being 70 cents a gallon and the highest being 85 cents a gallon at Eddontenajon, British Columbia. Looking back on it, I now realize what a bargain it was, although at the time it didn't seem that way.

My bull from "Big Lake."

Chapter Seven

STRANDED IN ALASKA

September found Joanne and I on a commercial flight back to Fairbanks, Alaska. As stated earlier, Wally Rochester and the crew at Clear, Alaska, had became pretty good friends and we looked forward to seeing them again. Wally had purchased a large church since we'd last been up there and had converted it into his hunting lodge. He and his wife lived in the "parsonage" at Rochester Lodge. Wally had turned the main portion of the church into a large trophy room where he displayed his many trophies including several polar bears, grizzlies, moose, caribou and several Dall sheep. This large room was also used for some dances, meetings, political gatherings and some wild parties like I'm sure that church had not seen in its past. Alaska's governor, Jay Hammond, hosted a political gathering there one time. The many small "Sunday school rooms" that were adjacent to the main room, Wally used for the hunters bedrooms. Joanne and I had one many times. Wally used to say that if he couldn't make the place pay its own way as a hunting lodge he could always turn it into a house of ill repute and those little Sunday school rooms would surely come in handy. Knowing Wally, I think he was at least halfway serious.

Joanne and I were met at the Fairbanks Airport by Wally and his wife and taken south the 80 miles to their new lodge where we set up and talked, drank and got reacquainted with each other.

The next morning (but not too early) as the crew was getting ready to take the two big track rigs out to their moose camp Wally asked me if I wanted to go look around a bit while we were waiting on the guys to pack the track rigs. "Sure, let's go!" He told me to grab my rifle and we'd go up in his "Super Cub" and see if there were any moose in the area. He had his plane on floats and was keeping it in a little float pond about four to five miles up the road. We were soon packing the necessary things in the plane and I climbed in the back seat and Wally got in the front for what was to be my first ride in a bush plane. An unforgettable experience! He taxied a short ways and we were in the air and looking down at the highway we had just driven up. We went out west of his lodge, across three pretty good sized rivers and had seen cows, but no bull moose. Wally was flying about two hundred feet elevation most of the time. He said he was afraid of heights. In later years I heard Wally say that if he was much over 300 feet up, he couldn't hardly see the ground.

We were approaching a lake that Wally said was "Big Lake" when I happened to spot a fair sized bull moose below us and right near the edge of a small pond. He was actually out in the water 50 feet or so feeding. I pointed him out to Wally and he circled around to get a better look and the next thing I knew we were dropping down over Big Lake and preparing to land on the water (another first for me). Wally made a good smooth landing and taxied over to the beach right by a small island and cut the engine. We tied the plane to some willows and he told me to grab my rifle and we'd go check out that bull.

The pond the bull was in was about one-half to three-quarters of a mile away through the muskeg. When we got near it the bull became aware of us and started to leave the pond. Wally said to wait until he had left the water and was on dry land before I shot. He did not want to butcher that big old bull in the water and mud. Apparently he'd done that before. When I thought the bull was only in three to four inches of water I shot him. Damn, but those critters have long legs! He was still in about twelve to fifteen inches of water and Wally wasn't too pleased with that, but he was down.

We got the butchering done in about fifteen to eighteen inches of water and mud. Now I understood Wally a whole lot better. We had brought our packboards out with us so now we each took a load back to the plane. As long as I knew him, Wally had a very bad back so he actually took a fairly small load, while I was young and dumb and had quite a large one to cross that muskeg with. The bending over and butchering had been rough on his back too. When we got to the plane we took everything out to make room for the meat that Wally was going to fly back to the float pond, about 40 miles east of our location. I always make sure I have a sleeping bag with me and this was no exception; I'd brought mine in the very back tail section of the super cub. I took it out to make room for the meat. I checked and made sure I had matches and a small water bottle, and of course my rifle. I had on a down coat and there was most of a package of fig bars in one pocket of it. I loaded the meat as per instructed and poor Wally would have the job of lifting it out of there when he got back to the float pond. Not an easy job! The plan was for me to return to the kill site for another load of meat while Wally flew this load the approximately 40 miles back to the float pond, unloaded it into his pickup and returned for another load. It took me awhile to prepare another load for the pack board and packing across the muskeg was not easy. I was sitting at the edge of the lake when I heard the super cub coming back. Wally had gotten the meat unloaded OK, but his back was starting to bother him more. He also said that the weather was starting to change and the flight had been a little bumpier that he and I had experienced. If my memory serves me right he made four round trips telling me each time that the air was getting rougher. After the last load of meat it was getting rather late and we were both very tired and he said that he'd just unload the meat and come right back for me.

Right next to where I waited for him was a very small island that I could actually wade out to. I had to wade about 125 feet and the water

My make-do camp at "Big Lake."

wasn't even over my knees, so I waded out to have a look around. It was obvious that someone had had a camp there before and abandoned it as there were four to five old cots that were in pretty sad shape along with a ripped up tent. The bears had really been rough on things here. I found several cans of what had been food with teeth punctures in them. The cots looked like the bears had tried tap dancing on them. There was an abundance of nylon cord, plastic kitchen utensils and cans.

When it started to get sort of dark I was glad I'd brought my sleeping bag along. I picked out the cot with the smallest holes in it and figured if worse came to worse I'd sleep right there on that little island and not suffer too much as there were some pretty big scraps of the old tent too. I ate about half of my fig bars and even found a jar of "Taster's Choice" instant coffee. The bears had tried unsuccessfully to bite it but actually did it no harm. You could see their tooth marks on the jar where their teeth had just slipped off the glass. That was the first time I'd even heard of "Taster's Choice" and I don't care much for instant coffee. It seems to me it's like a kiss on the forehead, it just doesn't do much for me. But I do like my morning coffee so things weren't looking too bad. When it got dark enough that I was sure Wally would not be in that night I spread my sleeping bag on that old cot and soon was sound asleep. Quite tired after the butchering and packing! I knew Wally would be back in the morning if the weather was halfway decent.

Fig bars and coffee don't make too bad of a breakfast. Even if it is instant coffee! I spent the morning anxiously awaiting the sound of that little super cub, but it didn't happen. It got to be a long afternoon and I knew Joanne would be getting concerned about me being out there alone. When it started to become late in the afternoon I decided I'd better make another trip out to where I'd killed the bull and see if I couldn't find some "usable scraps" to roast over a fire as I was getting hungry. I picked up my rifle, waded to the shore and returned to the site. There actually was quite a lot of usable scraps and would have been a lot more if it weren't for the birds that had been sitting and roosting on it. They'd eaten some, but had ruined more. There was still enough for me to take back and cook over the little fire I built though. No more fig bars, but moose meat and coffee ain't too bad either. I even brought back more meat than I thought I'd need, just to keep it from those dirty birds. I spent the afternoon wondering where Wally was and why he hadn't showed up yet. Ate a little more moose meat and crawled in the sleeping bag for the second night on the little island. Surely he'd be here tomorrow!

Wally's Super-cub with a load of moose meat.

I couldn't have too big a fire as wood was not very plentiful or close. Nothing near except a few small dead alders about two to three inches diameter near the water's edge. There was some old white gas in a broken Coleman lantern that I used to get the fires going. Kinda handy! By this time I'll admit, I was getting concerned. Where in the heck was Wally? Had his plane crashed? Or was the weather just too rough to fly? I really doubted the latter because the weather seemed pretty good to me. Rather windy and cool, but certainly not anything to prevent flying. If he had crashed, did anyone know where I was? Had he had a chance to tell them? What was going through Joanne's mind? If he's not here today I'd better start walking east. All I have to do is head straight east and I'm bound to hit the highway between Fairbanks and Anchorage. I think I should be able to cross those three rivers because like most of them up here, they are multi-channeled. Probably not easy but I can't just sit here and wait if nobody knows where I am.

No, I better not do that. Everything I've ever read says to stay put and you'll be found. Don't go wandering off. That would be foolish! Just wait! God helps those who help themselves, so I better start in the morning. No, they'll start a search in a few days and I'll just flag down a plane and then I'll find out what happened to Wally.

Talk about undecided! A lot goes through your mind in a situation like that. One minute I'd want to wait and the next I knew I should start walking out. Forty miles shouldn't be too hard to do. Beats sitting here not knowing!

I slept the third night on the island. The next day I tried to catch one of the big fish that were in the reeds near the shore of the island. I think they were pike. Anyway, I failed miserably at that task. That evening I saw a small bull moose swimming the lake and he was coming right for "my" island. I didn't want him running through camp as I'd stretched some of the nylon cord I'd found between two trees and hung part of the old tent over it for some shelter. When he got quite close I hazed him off. Then I made another meat run. I was out of meat, so back to the several days old kill site. The birds had done a number on the carcass and by this time my worries were added to because a bear had found it and eaten most of what had been left. I didn't spend much time there but grabbed some of the least dirty scraps and decided I'd clean them up at camp. I still had plenty of instant coffee though, but I was running low on matches. Where in the heck was Wally?

The next day wasn't much different than the rest of them except that I was getting more worried all the time; worried about Wally most of all, but also Joanne and myself. If only I knew what had happened! Joanne and I were supposed to go out behind Rochester Lodge to hunt and now with this situation, I didn't know where she would be. As it turned out she had gone to moose camp with the rest of the group and the cook, Porky, was watching out for her. My indecision was growing with each day. I wanted to try to walk out, but on the other hand I felt I should remain on the island. Worried, bored and undecided!

Early the next morning, I was much relieved to first hear and then see that black and white super cub preparing to land on the lake. Likewise, Wally was very relieved to find me still there and safe. He said that when he flew over the spot where I'd killed the bull there were two grizzlies there cleaning things up. Glad I didn't have to go back there that day. I soon learned that it had been way too windy and rough for him to fly at the lodge. He was merely waiting for good weather, which happens a lot up there. It was not nearly that bad where I was, strange how much difference forty miles can make. Wally and I flew directly to the camp bypassing the lodge, where I was met by a very happy wife. She told me later that Wally had been genuinely concerned about my safety there as he knew grizzlies would show up there sooner or later. All's well that ends well.

Chapter Eight

JOANNE'S BIG BULL

The year of 1977 was a very busy one for Joanne, me, and our family. I had bought another piece of property near our home. I logged most of the trees off it and then cleared the balance of it, seeding it into pasture for our horses. Then Joanne and I decided we would build a house on it to take advantage of the location (we loved it).

Anyone that has ever undertaken the job of building their own home knows how frustrating that can be. We worked long and hard on it. One very hot September day we were pouring concrete steps and sidewalks in front of the new house in mid-day and by evening we were on our way back up north to Fairbanks, Alaska, where Wally was to meet us again and for Joanne's moose hunt. That's right, she'd be doing the shooting this year. After our house building summer we really needed a break.

Wally met us and took us to the Lodge where we turned in right away as it had been a real long day. Try pouring concrete and then going to Alaska moose hunting, all in one day.

That reminds me of a sight we saw that day on the way to Alaska that we'd never seen before or since. We actually saw the sun set twice that day. We left the Portland airport in the early evening and flew to Seattle, where we landed for a short time. As we were setting down in Seattle the sun was just setting out over the Puget Sound. Very pretty! By the time we took off it was pretty dark outside. As we flew northwest for several hours I began to notice the western sky getting lighter all the time. Sure enough, when we got to Fairbanks the sun was just setting AGAIN. Of course the days are a lot longer in Alaska than here and we were going further west all the time, so that would explain it. It sure seemed odd to us though.

The next morning we only had a short time to wait while Les and

Myron performed a few last minute adjustments on the track rigs and then we were off to the moose camp. If I remember correctly it was seventeen to eighteen miles from the lodge into their moose camp. I do remember that it was a very wet and muddy trail across the muskeg and through the sparse spruce trees.

I usually rode along on the track rig with Joanne and Myron who was trying to find a bull for her. Porky, the camp cook, was their driver while Joanne and Myron and whoever was up on top of the large rig watching for moose. These big rigs were very quiet in the bush as that's the way the government had designed then. They were military surplus.

On the day that she got her bull, I'd gone with Les out to see if we could shoot a few ptarmigan for supper that night. The birds were quite plentiful. We heard some shots coming from the approximate direction that the others were supposed to be in. We headed over that way and it didn't take us too long to find them. Joanne had her bull alright, thanks to Myron's keen eyes. It was huge! Was she ever elated! Myron had spotted it and Joanne could just barely see it if she stood on her tiptoes. Well there are not too many ways to shoot a rifle that would be less conducive to good marksmanship than standing on your tiptoes. That

The author's wife, Joanne, and guide Myron Stokes with Joanne's 62-inch bull.

muskeg country is so flat that they were unable to maneuver the track rig around to help her. Myron could see the big bull, but Joanne could only see it by stretching. Needless to say it took several shots, but she did get it on the ground. We took quite a few pictures of her and her 62" moose. Joanne is also 62" tall, so it's easy to remember the width of her bull. Nowadays, her bull is in our den and mine resides in the basement, but that's okay. I'm glad she got it and very proud of her.

When we returned from Alaska we got back to work on the house and then moved into our new home December 4th, 1977. Incidentally, that new home, which we're still in, is on the adjoining property from that old one room school where I started the first grade. The old school and I are both still standing.

Loaded up and ready to head off to camp. Joanne holds her rifle and the antlers.

Looking for gold.

Chapter Nine

DALL SHEEP AND CARIBOU

In February of 1979 two of our children were involved in a terrible car wreck. It was nearly head-on and put them both in hospitals. Our youngest daughter, Carma, ended up in a hospital in Longview, Washington, not too far from our home, while Dan, one of our twin sons, ended up in the intensive care unit at a hospital in Portland, Oregon. This whole thing took quite a toll on the family, especially Dan. It was several days until the Dr. told us Dan would eventually make it. It was rough on us all with two kids in two separate hospitals in two different states fifty miles apart. Neither Jo nor I were able to go to work of course. We were busy trying to spend time at both hospitals and occasionally came home for a shower and to get clean clothes. When Dan was finally released from the hospital, he needed almost continual care from mom and also had frequent doctor and therapy appointments. He was not to go to work for many months.

I had an opportunity to go back to Alaska for a sheep and caribou hunt that fall ('79) and it seemed to me that after all Dan had been through he should have the chance to join me. He wasn't up to hunting yet, but I was sure he'd enjoy the trip anyway. I talked to Wally and made arrangements for Dan to stay at the lodge while I went sheep hunting with Les and Myron. Then when I returned from that, Les and I planned to take Dan with us while I hunted caribou.

Dan was very anxious to go to Alaska with me and I think it proved good therapy overall.

We were met, as usual, in Fairbanks by Wally and driven to Rochester Lodge and then the next day we started preparing for a sheep hunt (my first) in the Wood River area of the Alaska Range. Wally cranked up the little super cub and took Myron, Les and I and our gear into the mountains. This took three trips with a little of the gear with each of us. Wally had the cub on tundra tires now instead of the floats so we landed on a short strip that had a rise in it near the far end if you were landing or near the beginning if you were taking off. It was like a split level landing strip. But we made do, as always! Myron gave Wally a date to check on us and he returned to the lodge. Next we set up a small tent for our base camp and then proceeded to do some glassing. No sheep in sight, but tomorrow would be another day. It was so nice we threw our sleeping bags on our air mattresses outside of the tent that night and right after dark we were treated to a gorgeous display of the northern lights.

The next morning after a quick bite of breakfast we shouldered our packs and started a gradual climb up the mountain. It was really quite easy going here. I immediately began to notice all of the small quartz outcroppings in the area and was having a hard time concentrating on the climbing and sheep hunting. I'd have liked to investigate those little piles of quartz much closer; that has always been an interest of mine. We hadn't climbed too far before Myron spotted a lone, small ram on the other side of a valley we were paralleling . We got up just high enough so that our eyeballs cleared the top of the ridge and were able to determine that there were no more with him on THAT SIDE of the valley. Les said that the little ram may very well be a "lookout" for more sheep on our side of the valley that were still out of our sight. I guess he knew more about sheep than I did as he was absolutely correct. We began a slower, more watchful stalk and soon Les spotted more sheep bedded right on top of the ridge we were climbing. Luckily he saw them first.

In preparation for this hunt I had taken my Remington .30-06 auto to a local gunsmith to have it cleaned and given a good once over before my hunt. I had a four power Weaver scope on it. He advised me to take a flatter shooting bolt gun. I disagreed and told him I'd killed lots of game with that rifle, but not sheep. I had faith in it. Upon arriving in Alaska when I test fired it to see how bad the airport monkeys had abused it I was surprised to find it shooting quite a ways off. I corrected it, shot another shot or two and we went hunting.

As we proceeded on up the ridge towards the sheep, Les and Myron informed me that there was indeed a decent ram with the bunch and he was bedded among some huge boulders right on top of the ridge. They thought we could get real close if we were lucky, maybe even 75 yards or so. We had the wind in our face and the sheep didn't know we were even on the same mountain as them. We got about 50 yards when I

Friends and guides, Les Mortenson on the left and Myron Stokes with my Dall ram.

pushed the rifle barrel up over the top of the ridge and fired just as the ram stood up. I hit him, but it was a lousy shot, too far back. Because it was an automatic I immediately shot again, missing entirely as the ram hobbled towards the other side of the ridge. He was still less than 100 yards away when I finally grounded him. Terrible shooting! What the heck was happening? My first thought was the gunsmith that had advised against bringing the rifle.

After some pictures of my first ram we caped him and prepared to get back down to our spike camp. I was ashamed of my shooting.

The next morning I was awakened by something walking on the gravel ridgetop that we still had our sleeping bags on. I think I was the first to hear it and it took me a few seconds to locate the source as the big bull caribou was walking right towards our heads. That is an awkward position to see any thing from when you're still half asleep and in the bag. He was beautiful! He actually walked to within about 15 to 20 yards from us before he saw us. By that time Les and Myron were awake and we all got to see him. However we had no caribou tag for this area.

This camp was handy to the plane but very unhandy when it came to water. We were just about out of water, but could see a nice stream below us. It looked like about a 400 yard hike to the stream where we could wash up, get a drink and carry what water we could back up to our ridge top camp. Not much to do 'til Wally showed up and that would be a few more days. When we hiked to the creek we discovered an old cabin site. The little cabin had burned many years before. There were remains of a few hand tools laying next to where the cabin had stood. A shovel and axe lay nearby minus their handles. There were the remains of an old gasoline powered pump, a victim of the fire too. Finally we found the partial remains of a sluice box. Now we knew what the old cabin had been used for. Because we were in no hurry at all, we spent several hours looking around the claim. We found three corner markers and miscellaneous tools and junk. We also found color! It was not too difficult either. That old miner was sharp and knew his stuff because the stream had eons before cut through a low and long mound of earth here (like a dike) and consequentially the wide valley narrowed to only a few yards. This must have been very effective in slowing the water thus allowing the gold to settle out here.

All very interesting to us, and we had nothing but time! We found a short piece of old fire hose and cut it length ways and laid it out flat on

Wally Rochester and his Super-cub.

a piece of a 1x12-inch board we salvaged. By elevating one end of this crude apparatus we now had a mini-sluice box. I'd noticed the old shovel head earlier, so now we were in business. We scooped up some likely looking sand and carried it in the shovel head over to the board with the canvas covered fire hose on it. Slow process, yes! But it was fun and effective. If only we'd have had a few more tools and some equipment! You don't move much sand with only the head of a shovel. It wasn't long before we started to find little flecks of gold in the canvas covering of the old hose. I was so proud of it that I saved a little dust in a scrap of old tin foil and brought it home to show Joanne and the kids. Joanne laughed at the meager amount.

The next day we ventured back down for some more water and to do a little more mining with about the same results. That evening Wally came in and took us and the ram back to the lodge in three trips.

We now planned to take Dan with us and go after a caribou bull, but the first thing I did was to go to a local gravel pit and shoot my '06 to try and find out why I'd done such a lousy job of shooting. It was way off again, but after several shots I thought I had it pretty close so we drove down to the Denali highway near where Jo and I had been six years earlier in '73. We hired Butch Gracious from the Gracious House Lodge

Author and son, Dan, with caribou racks.

to fly Dan, Les and I up onto a place called Pony Ridge where we set up our tent. There weren't many caribou in the area but on the second day there we managed to see several and while Dan watched from camp, Les and I made a stalk on a decent bull. Not real big, but decent enough for my first caribou. In the final stage of the stalk we ended up on our bellies, crawling several yards to get a shot at the unsuspecting bull. Les was behind me and carrying his left handed .270 also. When I fired I knew I'd hit the bull but it was not a good shot and the next one missed entirely. I turned and took Les's rifle and killed the bull. What in the heck was wrong with mine? Later that day Les got a bull also and the next day Butch came by to check on us, but ended up landing and taking us and our meat and antlers all out and back to the Denali highway.

When we got back to Rochester Lodge the first thing I did was to grab my '06 and some shells and head back to that gravel pit to shoot the gun and try to find the problem. Every time I'd shoot it would hit a different spot. There was no adjusting it. When I got home a few days later I sent it back to the Weaver factory and they replaced the loose crosshairs. That explained why I couldn't seem to really get it sighted in and why the next shot was always in a different spot.

Chapter Ten

PACKING INTO THE SELWAY-BITTERROOT WILDERNESS

We had always had our own horses and mules around home as our kids and I enjoyed riding. Our daughters, Cathy and Carma, were more interested than our sons, which is not unusual. I did a lot of trail riding near home and sometimes would trailer the horses up near Mt. St. Helens in Washington state and ride and camp there. I annually hosted about three dozen riders on an overnight ride near our home. The more I saw of this sort of thing, the more I enjoyed it, so the trips to the Selway-Bitterroot Wilderness in Idaho were a natural "next step" in September of 1981. We used to trailer our horses and mules to a trailhead west of Darby, Montana, and pack in from there. This would put us into the heart of the beautiful Bitterroot Mountains. As I've always loved the high country, I certainly did enjoy these trips. We'd pull our four-horse trailer the 17 miles into the trailhead, then unload and pack in to a remote spot we had found. Lots of good bulls there at that time and we always had a real variety of weather. It would be too hot to hunt when we arrived but quite often we'd pack out in the snow. In fact we always saw some snow there. On one trip the smoke was so thick from a nearby forest fire that we were unable to "glass" in the afternoons. In the mornings after the fire had died down in the night it wasn't too bad. Another time while camped in there with our friend, Bill, we were up way before dawn getting ready to go out hunting and had a wonderful experience. While we were saddling the horses we noticed the northern lights shimmering in the northern skies. If to add to that great sight, meanwhile we heard a bull elk bugling in the canyon below. WOW!!

On our first trip in there, our local veterinarian, Jeff, wanted to accompany Joanne and I. He was not too interested in the elk hunting but was in need of some time away from his office and the telephone. We had a good time and I learned a lot of country, but we never shot anything. In future pack trips in there we were joined by friend Bill Williams twice, our daughter, Carma, and son-in-law, Bill Harrel once. On still another trip our son, Dave, and my hunting partner of many years, Dale Trautman, packed in with us. It was Dave's first time at this type of a hunting trip. He learned a lot! On this particular trip I had killed a 5x5 bull and Dale and I would pack it out to the truck very early the next morning while Dave kept on hunting. Then we'd unload it into the truck and unsaddle, feed and tie the stock while we made the 17 mile trip out to the highway and then the 15 mile trip to a cooler in town. We also had a short grub list that Joanne had given me. I'd shop while Dale called home. All of this was done with a few inches of snow on the ground. Then, of course , we had to make the return trip to the trailhead, saddle up and try to get back to camp before it got too dark or too late. We'd told Joanne and Dave that if we could leave the trailhead by 4:30 p.m. we'd ride in that night. If it got later than that they could expect us the

Our Selway Wilderness camp.

next morning and not to worry. We hurried all day and it was about 4:45 when we stepped up into the saddles that afternoon. On the return trip to our camp that evening we were treated to one of the most unforgettable experiences I've ever witnessed. As it started to get along toward dusk we started to hear bull elk bugle. The darker it got the more bugles we heard. It was also getting very chilly as we rode on through the snow and into the night. There would be a full moon that night thus enabling us to find the trail to camp. As we approached the summit of those beautiful Bitterroots, with that full moon and about eight inches of snow on the ground we turned the horses around to look out over the prettiest part of Montana while being serenaded by several bull elk in the light of a full moon. Folks, it just doesn't get any better than that! It was hard to turn away and leave that sight.

Over the years I've hunted several areas in the Bitterroot Mountains, but this camp was my favorite. We took a few bulls from there and a few in other parts of that mountain chain, but never any real big ones. Always enjoyable though!

One of our Selway bulls with Duane and Joanne.

My bull from the Jicarilla.

Chapter 11

ELK HUNTING ON THE JICARILLA

It was in the late fall of 1982 when my longtime friends from Alaska and I decided to venture to New Mexico's famed Jicarilla Indian Reservation near Chama to hunt elk. Les Mortenson and Bert Kawati arrived at my home right after Christmas of '82. We spent a day or so getting organized and then packing my '79 Ford pickup for the long trip south. The weather forcast was favorable, so very early on the last day of 1982 we left for New Mexico. We spent a very quiet, calm, boring "New Years's Eve in Salt Lake City, Utah. Not the most exciting place in the world to be on New Year's eve! When we checked into a motel there Les asked where we could go to buy a few beers to bring back to our room and the guy behind the counter got a blank look on his face and finally tried to remember where the nearest liquor store was. It turned out in was clear across town, but we found it just before they closed, which was quite early, but I don't remember the exact time.

We had made arrangements to hunt with a fellow by the name of Ronnie Demasters out of his home in Chama. He was the only white man at that time who had permission from the Indians to hunt the reservation.

The first day we were asked about our preferred way to hunt and it was explained to us that going horseback would be the most productive as those elk were very used to the Indians shooting at them from vehicles. Les and I chose the horseback route while Bert opted to take his chances from the pickup truck. The first day produced nothing for any of us. The second day my guide and I headed for some higher country and more snow. In fact we were near the Continental Divide when Ronnie suggested we tie up the horses and proceed on foot. Whew, I soon realized there was an oxygen shortage in that part of New Mexico. It's a good thing there weren't more than just he and I because I don't think there would have been enough air for a third person. We'd have needed to take turns breathing. I finally got to the top of this little ridge and we continued to walk north on it a half mile or so when I spotted a decent bull down below us. My first shot put him down and the second one kept him there. When we finally got down to him I found him to be just a good big 5x5 bull, nothing huge, but nice. We skidded him to the truck with a horse and rope. A couple of nights later when looking at a map we discovered that I'd killed him from the top of the continental divide. The bull was on the east side however.

The next day Bert and his guide came in with the monstrous big 6x6 that Bert had shot. Yes, while hunting from the road in a pickup! So much for the Demasters theory! The following day Les got an average 4x4 bull so we stayed one more night and then headed home.

The roads were still good when I started out driving. Bert had wanted breakfast but Les and I were anxious to get started so Les had gone to a local mini-mart and grabbed a sack of junk food and some sandwich makin's while Bert and I loaded the meat and horns with the help of Ronnie. Bert whined and hollered about being hungry while Les

Author at the left, Bert in the center and Les Mortenson with the Jicarilla bulls.

and I ate a sandwich and had a cup of coffee from the Thermos bottle. He said he needed a big breakfast. I kept driving. Bert went to sleep. When he woke up we were only about 15 miles or so from the Four Corners area between Utah, Colorado, New Mexico and Arizona. Unknown to Les and I, we had passed the junction where we'd needed to turn north. Only a few miles back, but nonetheless we'd missed it! Bert wanted to drive so I let him. We only went a few miles before we saw the signs welcoming us to the "Four Corners" area. We all knew that we didn't want to be there and quickly figured out that we'd missed our turn north. Bert turned around after we viewed the Four Corners and we headed east. Les and I began to give Bert a bad time about his not paying attention to the road signs. We told him that if he was going to drive he'd have to watch for signs and follow them. He agreed and took it good. Truth is he never did find out that I was the one who'd missed the turn shortly before he started driving. We continued to razz him about that 'til the day he died and he never knew it was not his mistake.

When we got home I took my 5x5 to the taxidermist, and Les took his antlers home while Bert left his with my son, Dave, to put on a plaque. At the time Dave and Renay were newly married and living in a

Tribal officer talking to Ronnie DeMasters.

single wide trailer home. Bert's elk was so wide that Dave was unable to get it down the hallway in his trailer to mount it on the plaque. A fun trip with two good friends! It was fun teasing Bert. Incidentally, Bert pulled into the very first restaurant he came to and we had to take time out to eat a meal.

Chapter Twelve

MULE DEER IN IDAHO

In the summer of 1986 I suggested an Idaho mule deer hunt to our daughter and son-in-law, Carma and Bill. I'd been doing some research on a couple of areas in southeastern Idaho. Carma had never killed a mule deer and neither Bill nor I had ever killed one that met our hopes and expectations. Joanne and I had taken a road trip the previous summer and had our choices narrowed down to two or three places.

The second spot we chose was the one we agreed had possibilities of enabling us to fill our tags with good bucks. The roads into it were horrible (that cuts down on the competition). We spotted lots of deer right off. Lots of just average bucks! We had taken two pickups and a trailer with two Honda four-wheelers in it. The trucks were filled with a large tent, our kitchen, groceries, gas and gear. We were ready! We left the highway with tire chains and went in about one and a half miles where we unloaded the four-wheelers and Bill and I rode up to locate a spot to camp. Next we proceeded another mile and a half to little flat spot to pitch the tent. There we parked the trucks 'til we were ready to go home as the roads were too steep and rutted for them. After setting up camp we had only enough time to make a quick run up a couple roads to try and help us decide where to start hunting the next morning.

This was in the days when four-wheeled ATVs were still pretty new so we had almost no competition up on these mountains. Sorry to say that it's not that way now in this area or most others.

We found an area about five miles from our camp that suited us and we could always find deer in a certain long, steep, rugged canyon up there. We usually saw a couple dozen deer while riding the four-wheelers up there to hunt. We do not hunt from these machines but only use them to get out to the chosen area and then to haul game back to the truck.

About the third or fourth day on a very cold, single digit morning when Carma was sitting at the edge of a small clearing alone she witnessed several small bunches of deer occasionally flowing through the clearing. There was about four to five inches of snow on the ground and the sun was NOT shining into this little valley. She sat very still as a large doe trotted down off the ridge and entered the small meadow where she sat. She was being followed and courted by a lone monster mule buck. Carma was shooting a little 7x57 rifle that I'd bought for her. I'm proud to say that she kept her wits about her enough to get a couple of

Author's daughter, Carma Harrel, with her 33½-inch Idaho buck.

shots into that big buck and she had him laying on the ground when her husband showed up. Her first mule deer! Back at camp the buck measured 33½ inches wide. He was a 5x7 with several more "almost" points. We were proud of her. Bill ended up with a small buck and Joanne and I came home empty-handed as we didn't see any bucks quite big enough.

The following year we took our good friend, Tim Combs, in there with us. As we arrived after dark and because it was dark when we left camp the next morning, I told Tim that he could have my favorite "early morning stump". Joanne and I would go elsewhere until about 10:30 when we'd come back to get him and show him around the country. We were about a half mile from him and were sitting about 200 yards apart when we heard Tim shoot several times. Along about 10:00 we made our way up there just in time to see Tim loading his 37½-inch 4x4 buck on his ATV. What a monster! Tim is a good friend and a very ethical sportsman, which he has proven by not going back there since. More than I can say for a lot of guys I know!

Over the next few years we took other family and friends in there but nobody ever topped Tim's or Carma's bucks. Our son, Dan, and his wife went along one year as did our good friends, Dale Trautman and Steve Chambers. We all killed bucks, but not the big ones we were hunting. Tim Combs, Joanne and I had the pleasure of seeing six bucks there on the same hillside at one time that were over 30" wide. (But seeing them and shooting them are two different things entirely.) I used to pack a small two man tent about half a mile up on a ridge there along with enough sandwiches for one and a half days when the rut was on and the weather was right and had some great hunting there. When you add up the total mileage that I was in from the highway it gave me a real advantage. When I'd crawl out of the tent in the morning I could watch the other hunters headlights as they left the highway about five to six rough miles below me.

Tim Combs and his 37½-inch Idaho muley.

As I sit here now I can look up and see pictures of Tim and his buck and also Carma and us with her big one. Great memories, all!

Joanne with a nice Idaho mule deer.

One of my spike camps and the pay-off.

Chapter Thirteen

MORE B. C. HUNTS

The autumn of '87 found me on my way north once more to hunt in southeastern British Columbia for mountain goat and elk with my good friend, Bob Fontana, and his outfit, "Elk Valley Outfitters". Along with me was a client of ours from Longview, Washington.

By this time the booking agency we had started a couple of years earlier was getting better established and I wanted to actually hunt with Bob's outfit myself before sending future clients there. We had, by this time, signed on several corporate "clients" as customers and were rightfully very concerned about which outfitter they hunted with. Among these companies were Leupold/Stevens and also the Nosler Bullet Company. Leupold had previously given Joanne and I a guided tour through their factory followed by a nice dinner where we proceeded to explain our interests in placing hunters for them. They, like Nosler, sometimes sent special sales people, distributors or contest winners on hunting trips. This is where we came in. We counted John and Bob Nosler among our satisfied clients as well as Chub Eastman of Leupold (and later on, Nosler Bullets).

The client from Longview (Dale) and I pulled into Bob's headquarters on the Elk River in nice clear fall weather. After spending one night there in one of the cabins we packed several miles by horseback through an old burn into a large log cabin that we'd use as a base for our hunt. The clear weather soon left us and fog and a little wet snow took its place. On about the second day that I hunted we sat quite high up a mountain side waiting for the low fog to lift. We'd ridden horseback up into the ravine below us and as soon as the fog lifted we took off up the mountain. We immediately started seeing goats. They were either in an inaccessible spot, too far away or not of trophy size though. Finally the guide spotted a very large billy laying far above us on

Outfitter Bob Fontana, a friend we miss.

a narrow little bench. He was laying right on the edge, so the guide asked if I thought I could anchor him right there with my custom made Dave Gentry rifle in .375 H&H magnum. I felt that I could make the steep uphill shot, and did. At the shot the goat slumped in his bed and never moved ... for a few seconds. Then he slowly gave a little kick and rolled off the ledge. And rolled over ever so slowly, again and again and again until he finally stopped rolling about 300 yards from where he started. He never did roll fast, in fact I took two pictures of him as he rolled past me, but it was just too steep to try to stop a 300-pound carcass. When he finally stopped and we were able to climb down to him, sadly my suspicions were confirmed. He had "broomed" off both horns while rolling down that mountainside like a white beer keg. The guide said that I'd just been beat out of the record book.

A couple of days later Dale was able to get an average sized bull elk and we headed home.

I went back to that area several times to try my luck on a big elk and deer and although I got game, the big ones always seemed to elude me. It was on an elk hunt there that I first met Gary Bogner, future SCI president, as we shared a cabin before his sheep hunt and my elk hunt.

Later on in life we were destined to meet again and we remain friends to this day. On that elk hunt I ended up killing an average sized bull about 150 yards west of the Alberta-British Columbia border, which is of course the "Continental Divide". So, this meant that I had now killed two bull elk from the Continental Divide, one in New Mexico and one in Canada. We had been hiking north along the border with its occasional cement markers when the guide decided to peer over into the head of a small canyon on the B.C. side and spotted the bull which I was able to knock down quite easily.

On another trip there I took both a mule deer and a whitetail deer. Bob and I remained friends until the day he was killed in Africa by a huge Cape buffalo.

Author with his mountain goat after it rolled off the mountain.

Duane with a British Columbia mule deer.

Chapter Fourteen

QUEBEC CARIBOU HUNT (1988)

In the mid 1980s Joanne and I had started a small hunt booking service (North-West Hunting) out of our home. As far as I know it was the first of its kind in Oregon, although now it seems there is one in nearly every city. We offered several hundred big game hunts to sportsmen and traveled to outdoor shows and expositions in the western U.S. We only exhibited at one show back East and that was in Nashville, Tennessee, although we considered doing a show in Pennsylvania several times. These shows were quite successful for us and many of our clients became friends for life. It seems like wherever we go we encounter clients from the past and usually end up in a long conversation about old times and other hunts.

On one of these hunts we were putting together it became apparent that we should do the hunt ourselves. We had been sending clients to Quebec for caribou hunts with Jack Hume and now we would make the trip too. Mike and Jeanette Brusco from Longview, Washington, and Tim Combs and Monty Crews from White Salmon, Washington, would join us.

So in August of 1988 we flew to Montreal, over-nighted there, and early the next morning boarded a big charter plane to Schefferville, Quebec, a desolate town in the northeastern portion of the country. There we met our outfitter, Jack Hume, who issued us licenses, ushered us to the local grocery store so we could buy supplies as this would be a self-guided trip although Jack would have a hired hand in our camp to help with camp chores, do the capeing and run the small boat that was there. After that we were taken to the bunk house where we were told that we'd be picked up early the next morning for the final bush plane flight to our hunting camp. We had the entire place to ourselves that night and it was indeed a very happy bunch of hunters.

We got up early the next morning and were crammed into an Otter with all our gear for the 130 mile flight to our caribou camp. It was very rainy and windy so we flew low, which gave us the chance to watch the ground for caribou.

No sooner had the big Otter banked and landed on the lake in front of our camp and we were busy unloading our gear when someone spotted caribou swimming the lake. Talk about excitement! The gear was still piled on the beach, the plane hadn't even left yet, our rifles were still stowed in their shipping cases, and the bolts for some were in separate boxes. Who knew where the ammunition was! Everyone was hollering to get somebody after the big bull that was in the smallest herd swimming to our side of the lake. The lake was nearly a mile across, but caribou make short work of that distance, either in the water or on land. Somehow it was decided that Joanne would be the one to go for him. The camp guide (I'd later learn his name was Zoel) would transport her to a point of land about a mile from camp, hopefully ahead of the bull. Time was of the essence, so once she unpacked her rifle, found her shells and her binoculars, Joanne and Zoel were off after the big bull. For me to

Tim Combs carries out a caribou rack.

accompany her and aid in any way would be out of the question as it would slow the boat too much. They were off in a spray of water with the last minute instructions to wait 'til he gets clear out of the water before shooting, take careful aim and shoot 'til you know he's dead and don't shoot if he's not quite what you want. Talk about getting off to an exciting start!

Somewhere along the line the plane departed for Schefferville as we watched the boat's progress. It was a very close race but the caribou won by a nose. He hit the beach at a dead run. Since she couldn't get a shot, Joanne and Zoel returned to camp. When they got back we introduced ourselves to Zoel and then started moving into our "home". We hadn't even seen the inside of the large tent that was to house us.

We had just gotten a good start moving in when someone announced another herd of caribou was crossing the lake, so our move-in ceased again. No decent bulls this time so back to unpacking and rolling out the sleeping bags, when guess what? More caribou, but only cows, calves and young bulls this time, but they were still exciting to watch.

Once we finally got settled in everyone grabbed their rifle and

A happy caribou camp. From left are Monty Crews, Mike Bruso, Zoel, Tim, Duane and Joanne.

This is the way Joanne likes to hunt caribou.

headed out to get acquainted with the country and the caribou. It was about 9:30 a.m. on the first day of our six day hunt and we'd already seen many caribou right from camp. Things were looking pretty good!

Tim and Monty took off on foot up the big river right behind camp, while Zoel took the rest of us up the lake with Jo and I getting out about a mile from camp and Mike and Jeanette going to the far end of the lake.

Caribou were swimming almost continually but no big bulls were spotted until just before dark when a real good one with long beams and good bez tines swam across and landed about 100 yards from us. We'd already decided that Joanne would try for him as soon as he hit the beach. This was the biggest caribou she had ever seen and when the opportunity came for a shot she got bull fever and shot way low. It was hard for her to do a good job of shooting with those huge antlers in her scope. Zoel picked us up a few hours later. I wished Joanne better luck in the morning.

The second day of the hunt found Tim with a real good bull and Monty came in late that day with a small one. As is so easy to do, he'd misjudged and thought the bull was much larger. We had indeed broken the ice. Much to my satisfaction, things were looking good. Caribou hunting is usually a feast or famine situation no matter how much planning you do.

Day three produced a very large bull for Jeanette. While she sat by a small fire eating cookies and drinking coffee a good bull wandered by and presented a good broadside shot. Mike came up just as she shot and waded the river to retrieve her bull. Jeanette helped too, she held his clothes.

That afternoon I changed locations and had some of Monty's luck. A bull fed slowly toward me until he got my scent and then he whirled and ran. One shot dumped him in his tracks. Closer inspection showed his horns to be smaller than I had expected. I would have sworn that bull was larger when I shot.

The fourth day was a good one. Tim and Monty each bagged their second bull and Joanne had recovered from her bull fever and shot a bull

From left are Jeanette, Mike, Joanne, Duane, Tim and Monty with 11 bulls.

at about 125 yards. It too was across the river, but unlike Mike, I waited 'til Zoel showed up with his hip boots on to wade over and retrieve it. Our time was running out. We only had two more days to hunt.

Mike and Jeanette changed areas on the fifth day and lucky Jeanette encountered a big bunch of bulls, picked out a nice one with double shovels and shot it with her trusty .270. Mike, who heard the shot showed up again in time to cross the river and retrieve her bull. The remaining bulls were just leaving, but not fast enough as Mike downed his first bull. It was a real nice caribou that he was unable to better. About this time Joanne found one that suited her and she managed to kill it with one shot. Now she had both of hers and was content to watch the rest of us attempt to limit out. Not bad, three bulls on the fifth day.

Only one more day for Mike and I to hunt for our second trophies! I did manage to take another that last day although it wasn't as big as I'd hoped for. Mike hunted 'til dark but failed to find the one he wanted, so we ended up with eleven bulls in six days. What a great sight to see those eleven sets of caribou horns lying on the beach in front of our camp. The northern lights flickering overhead and reflecting in the lake only served to add to the contentment. It had been a successful hunt shared with good people and with reluctance we boarded the big Otter the next morning to start our long journey homeward.

Chapter Fifteen

ONCE IN A "LIFETIME" TWICE

Although a father seldom tolerates his son calling him crazy, I was not only tolerating it but I was rather amused by this outburst from Dave, my 28-year-old son. We had spent a considerable amount of time putting a sneak on one of Oregon's most prized big game animals, the California Bighorn sheep. After the successful stalk when I was ready to turn and leave, my son Dave, exclaimed, "You're crazy dad!" I found this amusing because I now realized that he wanted a sheep as much as I did. However I had hunted sheep several times before and knew how enjoyable it could be. I liked it too much to take this fine ram when the season was only a couple of hours old. I also knew we had a good chance of seeing many more rams and possibly even a bigger one. In contrast, Dave was looking at his first sheep.

As we turned to leave, I realized how lucky I was. Oregon's sheep tags are available through a drawing and are limited to one in a lifetime. Well, after years of applying in Oregon and most other western states and cashing more refund checks than I care to remember, I was finally able to pass up this coveted trophy and keep looking. I was finally sheep hunting in Oregon and by gosh we weren't going to take the first ram that came tripping down the trail. Further more I had an ace up my sleeve. I had also drawn an Idaho sheep tag for the following month. Again, a once in a lifetime tag (1988 was great!).

Dave was having trouble understanding my decision, as was Jim Usher, my son-in-law and our horse wrangler for the hunt. He didn't say much, just looked at me with an open mouth. My good friend and sheep guide, Elvin Hawkins of "Spot Country Outfitters" understood though. Elvin and I had been friends for several years and I'd told him several times that if I ever drew an Oregon sheep tag, he and I were going hunting. This was before he ever started his "Spot Country Outfitters". We saw more sheep on that opening day in September of '88 and passed up 15 rams.

We were hunting on Hart Mountain National Antelope Refuge in south-central Oregon, where there were six tags for the first season and six more for the second season. I had drawn my tag for the second season (Sept. 24 through Oct. 2, 1988).

It was late that first night by the time we rode off the mountain, loaded our horses and mules in the trailer and headed back to our camp in a remote campground. It had been a very long but highly enjoyable day. We had eaten breakfast at 2:30 a.m., had fed and saddled the stock and then had to drive an hour and a half to where we would park our rigs. Then we rode an hour to get to where we wanted to hunt.

The following day was almost a repeat of the first, except we hunted a little closer to camp and saw fewer rams. The third day was highlighted by Elvin almost walking into a rattlesnake that was hidden in a sage bush. The road we were traveling was so rough that while easing over a boulder we bent an axle on one of the horse trailers so that it toed in against the trailer frame. We had to unload the stock and overload the other trailer in order to get back to camp. It seemed like it took hours to get back that night, trailer tires rubbing all the way. We were one tired bunch when we pulled into camp that night.

On day four we left camp a lot later and tried a different area of Poker Jim Ridge. We managed to see a few rams but none were quite what we were looking for so we kept going. Suddenly Dave spotted two rams that were high above us and were scrambling up over a little ridge. They would have to cross a big bench on the side of the mountain before we could possibly see them again. After a quick discussion we decided to try to gain some altitude in hopes of seeing them again.

We climbed about 600 yards to a good vantage point before Dave again spotted the rams. One was bedded on a large boulder and the other was standing guard in some tall sagebrush. Both were fairly decent rams that we figured would score about 158 Boone and Crockett points. One was heavily broomed and Elvin and I both took a sudden liking to him. Dave favored the ram with the unbroomed headgear.

Neither ram was as large as the ram I'd passed up the first day, but it was now the fourth day and Dave and Jim would have to leave after two more days of hunting, plus we had a horse trailer in need of extensive repair. Dave was packing the video camera and getting what just might be the finale also had to be considered. All of these things kept bouncing around in my head and I finally told Elvin that we'd try to put a sneak on them and if it worked, I'd be taking the broomed off ram home with me.

The stalk took about an hour and then we had to wait about 45 minutes for the ram to stand up. We were as close as we could get – about 425 yards away. Elvin helped me build a rest for my 7mm Remington magnum. I placed my day pack on a large boulder, settled the rifle in, moved some rocks to sit comfortably and started the wait. Dave and Jim were behind some other boulders and were glued to their binoculars. Elvin and I went over the details: don't shoot until he gets up and turns broadside, and don't get mixed up and shoot the wrong ram. After looking at him through my 3-9 power scope and ranging him at 425 yards away I was confident I could take him in his bed if Elvin would just say the word. At that time I often target practiced at 300-600 yards.

When the ram finally stood up and turned broadside I was ready for him. That's why I was so surprised when Dave and Elvin both said that I'd missed the uphill shot. The elevation was correct but I'd shot to the

The author with son-in-law, Jim Usher, and son, Dave, with the author's ram.

Duane, son Dave and Joanne.

left, just missing him. The ram turned around, tried to find us and stopped again. I shot again. Same exact thing, a near miss to the left! In fact Elvin said it was so close he thought the bullet went right through the ram. When the ram started to run slightly to our left I knew I'd get another chance. About this time I realized that a slight breeze from right to left was the culprit. Anyway when I heard Dave holler and say "You got him, he's down" I was very relieved. Sure enough, he was shot through the neck. I had just bagged the fifty-first ram we had seen on the hunt.

It was a very happy sheep camp that night. The next day my ram was scored at 160 3/8 points – our Poker Jim ram, named after the ridge he was on was going home with us. Our joint efforts had paid off. Dave and Jim were hooked on sheep hunting and my wife Joanne was elated.

We returned home and I took "Poker Jim" to our taxidermist and three weeks later we were off to Idaho. I still had another sheep tag to fill.

The lower Salmon River was our destination – more precisely, the

Shepp Ranch on the Salmon. We were scheduled to hunt the last ten days of the season.

We were met at the end of the road by Mike Demerse for our trip by jet boat upriver to the ranch. We had thought our base camp at Hart Mountain had been nice, with our motor home and all the conveniences, but this place was fantastic. We had our own carpeted cabin with a fireplace, a shower, a kitchen and a big deck overlooking the beautiful River of No Return. There was also a hot tub and sauna – certainly not like the hunting camps we were used to.

Upon arrival, I was introduced to my guide for the next ten days, a young courteous fellow named Dave VonEsson. After we settled in he suggested that we head to the rifle range. I assured him I had just checked my rifle and scope and it was still sighted in. He insisted and I obliged and with that little chore out of the way we went out for an afternoon of sheep hunting leaving Joanne to lounge in that nice cabin. The country was steep and there was lots of it.

The next morning we settled into the daily routine of a big early breakfast and then a ride downstream by jet boat with Mike or Tommy to be let off for a days hiking, hunting and glassing. Later we'd be picked up at a prearranged spot for the ride back to camp.

Our daily trips enabled us to see a few small rams and ewes, a sow black bear and her two large cubs and lots of beautiful country but no legal rams. On the afternoon of the sixth day we were picked up early and we were informed of a large ram that had been seen near the river from the boat earlier that day. Just my luck; we were chugging up the mountains looking for the ram and he was down by the river.

We headed downstream and were able to spot the ram about 300 yards above the river. Before we got the boat to the beach, however, he was taking his three ewes up the mountain only to stop about 700 to 800 yards above the river. After a short council of war we decided there was not enough time to climb the steep ridge, shoot the bighorn, dress and cape him, pack him back down and still make it to the ranch by dark. Dave left it up to me and I suggested we come back the next day. I didn't think he'd be far away because the rut was just starting and these cliffs were home to the ewes.

After heading downstream at first light we beached the boat and began glassing. Finally Tommy spotted the ram's horns behind a rock not too far from where we'd seen him the night before, about 800 yards above us. Dave and I took off immediately after setting up some signals

The author glassing for sheep in Idaho's Salmon River country.

with Tommy.

We were able to stalk within 300 yards before a large muley buck noticed us and slightly spooked the sheep. As they started moving up and away, I needed a couple of minutes to get my breathing slowed down; then I looked at Dave and asked if he was ready with his binoculars. He nodded his approval and I took a good look through my scope and settled the crosshairs on the distant ram 300 yards away. He was very near the top of the ridge and partially hidden by a huge boulder. The single 165 grain handload entered his neck and severed his spinal column. I'm sure he never knew what hit him.

Dave let out a whoop that I'll never forget and Tommy was watching it all from the river. He saw the ram fall before he heard the shot.

After a few pictures and some happy chatter we caped the ram and Dave and I carried it the 400 yards or so to the river, arriving just in time to watch Tommy land a nice steelhead.

What a hunting season, two once-in-a-lifetime sheep tags. Both filled in the company of family and friends. Both were shot with the same rifle and scope combination. Both were shot in the neck at rather long distances. And they were bagged exactly one month apart – September 27th and October 27th, 1988.

As if that wasn't enough reason to celebrate, when we got back to the lodge I was informed that I had a new granddaughter. Stacy Dawn had been born a month early, but all was well. Grandma cried and I was one happy grandpa indeed. It was a season to remember.

The author and Joanne with sheep horns, the second in a month.

Chapter Sixteen

SAFARI TO SOUTH AFRICA

In June '89 we escorted a group of hunters to South Africa to hunt with one of the contacts that we had over there. Joanne and I were joined by Dick Crossley and his wife, Chris, from Tillamook, Oregon. We flew to Amsterdam where we had a day room to catch our breath, shower and rest a bit before leaving at midnight for Nairobi. From there, on to Johannesburg, South Africa, where we were met by our friends, Dan and Arlene Baugher, along with Rodney and Diane, all from Maryland. Also there to meet us was our Professional Hunter, Nico Pulsar, and guide Josh Van Stratton from Bushman Safaris. They drove us the four hours

From left are Duane, Joanne, and friend Peter Capstick.

north to the ranch where Dick, Chris, Joanne and I would stay while the "Maryland four" would travel on northeast in the following morning to hunt from still another camp.

The next time we would see them would be in Kruger National Park after our hunt was over.

A couple years earlier we'd had the good fortune of meeting and getting acquainted with Peter Capstick, who lived in South Africa. We jokingly mentioned hunting together some time, but this was not to be the time; in fact it never happened as Peter died an early death a couple of years later. I still have an autographed picture that he sent us on the wall of our den that we treasure (him holding up two huge elephant tusks). Also in our den you'll find the collector's edition of all his books which he signed and "personalized" to Joanne and I. Yes, we treasure them!

Joanne was the first in our group to take an animal when she killed a blesbuck the first morning. Later that day I got a warthog, which Jo said was "ugly". The next morning Joanne, I, Josh and our black tracker, Seelas, drove on north to a ranch owned by Dann Van De Heever where I'd hunt. This was a beautiful ranch right on the Limpopo River and hence on the Botswana Border. Botswana is a communist country. We hunted there about three days but always returned to the Bushman Safaris ranch at night. We usually left Bushman before daylight in order to arrive at the ranch on the Limpopo River in time to hunt at first light. About the third day of this Josh (who was one of the best guides we've ever had anyplace), informed us that we'd be leaving an hour and a half later the next morning as he had to drop his son off at school on the way. No problem! After we left the school and got on the dirt road near the ranch we were to hunt we met a very strange looking vehicle coming down the road. It was quite large and appeared to be pushing what looked to me like an old logging arch that used to be used in the logging industry back home. I asked Josh what it was and was astonished at his reply. It was a minesweeper used to detect land mines that the Botswana natives would occasionally place in the roads there when they'd cross the Limpopo River at night. WHEW!! We'd been driving that road each morning BEFORE the mine detector came through. Also, we'd been driving all of the roads on the ranch that were once in awhile mined too. Josh went on to tell us and show us several mine-proof cars that the ranch owners kept right by their door to enable them to get away fast and safe. What a way to live! Their yards were fenced with razor wire and they'd have the front gate opening and closing by a remote control in the car. No thanks! I did, however, get a real nice bushbuck here, along with a small eland and a good impala. Joanne said that she wanted an impala bigger than mine or Dick's and that is just what she got. Her 23+ inch impala placed 79th in the SCI record book. One thing that sticks in my mind about this beautiful place was the large, sweet oranges that they had on the stone table on the veranda there. They were bigger than a grapefruit and beyond comparison when it came to sweetness. I loved 'em! Another fond memory there, is of the deep fried bread she would make daily. Better than a doughnut! We enjoyed hunting on the Van De Heever farm with Josh and Seelas. We ate our lunch one day in a "wattle" hut. New experience for us! These huts are quite small and to "finish" them off, both the inside and the outside are smoothed over with fresh, very runny cow dung. The floor had a nice smooth finish to it just like a good cement floor might have.

One day we stopped by a neighboring farm to secure permission to hunt there. After that was agreed to, we were given directions to the black's encampment on the farm and instructed to go there and ask for a certain black tracker to aid us in my quest for a kudu. Upon arriving at their village where they were all outside cooking breakfast, we asked for the tracker. While he was preparing to go with us the little black kids

Dick Crossley with a nice Impala ram.

gathered around Joanne and began jabbering about her. The only word Jo caught was "Honky".

One night in the lodge Nico had told us all that he had to go to Johannesburg the next day to pick up two more hunters. Therefore we were not surprised the next night when we got back there and saw two new faces in the kitchen, but one continued to tax my memory and I noticed that he kept looking at me like he was trying to place me. As we were doing quite a few outdoor shows I did meet and see a lot of faces, so I finally asked him his name and where he was from. Allan Schwindt from Corvallis, Oregon, an artist that I'd seen in his booth at shows was now in the same house in South Africa with us. Small world, indeed! Allan and I went on to become friends and we remain so today with our trails crossing continually. He and his wife, Judy, now live in Washington state however.

After the hunt, Dick, Chris and Joanne and I were taken back to Johannesburg where we flew to Kruger Park to meet the other four in our group. After three days there we flew back to Jo'burg and then home.

Joanne and Duane with Duane's Limpopo bushbuck.

Chapter Seventeen

HUNTING ON OUR LEASE

By early 1990 we were trying to get away from booking hunters for other outfitters and decided to try something new and different. I originally leased just under 3,000 acres from International Paper Company near our home. I felt that with a little bit of help this land could become a real good place to hunt blacktails. When I did that, a neighboring landowner approached me about leasing his 600 acres also – so I did that too. Thirty six hundred acres of prime blacktail deer

The author with Dwight Schuh (center) and Larry Jones as they take a break from hunting Roosevelt's elk.

habitat to learn, study and hunt! During the preceding archery season I'd had 2 prominent archers stay at our home and hunt with me. Dwight Schuh and Larry Jones wanted some good Roosevelt elk hunting so came up and hunted with my son, Dave, and I. Some of the hunting we did was on this land that I later leased. Dwight ended up getting a nice bull. On the first day we hunted we just were not quite able to get within bow range of a huge bull. We never saw that one again.

We decided early on that we'd see just how good we could make the hunting here by limiting the number of hunters and also planting some of the newly logged areas with deer clover after we limed the soil. I also planted about 60 to 70 fruit trees throughout the lease. Next I bought an older camp trailer and parked on the lease for hunters to stay overnight in, make coffee in or dry clothes. I posted the land and it was close enough to my home so I was able to watch it quite closely. I built tree stands and towers to hunt from in various parts of the lease which enabled us to hunt in the re-prod where it is futile otherwise. We killed some nice four pointers this way. Steve Chambers says that he got spoiled there. We took some guided hunters but mostly it was for unguided hunters who'd hunted blacktail before. By limiting the number

Maryland hunters Arlene and Dan Baugher with Arlene's nice blacktail.

of hunters and restricting the vehicle traffic we were able provide some absolutely fantastic hunting. I still have a handwritten note here that our daughter, Carma, left at the trailer there for me. It said in part, "Dad, there are just too many bucks here. We saw two and on our way over to them we ran into several more that fouled our stalk". Over the few years we had the lease we had hunters from Alaska, Washington, Maryland, California, Utah, Montana as well as Oregon. One bunch of three that I especially remember was from Utah and they were not only nice guys but were also great hunters. One of them, Lou Dunyon and I are still friends and in fact we've hunted together in Arizona and Alaska since then. Lou is a man I greatly admire. Although not a monied man, he has hunted extensively, which just proves what I've always believed, "where there is a will, there is a way". Our good friend from Longview, Washington, Jeanette Brusco, loved hunting there and being the good hunter she is, she killed several nice bucks there. Jeanette liked it because of the fact that she never felt threatened there if she wanted to hunt alone.

Elk hunting was also pretty good there. The archers really liked it. I was surprised to learn that the bulls would bugle here up 'til about the

From left are Dale Trautman and Steve Chambers with their nice blacktail bucks.

Utah hunter Dave Myrup with his blacktail buck.

Washington hunter Dave Squires with a 4x4 blacktail.

25th of October or so, due to the fact that they were undisturbed. Dale Trautman and I disturbed some of them one day though, when we killed two nice bulls in one day.

But alas, all good things must come to an end. When International Paper Company sold off all of their land in Oregon, of course that went too. The new owners were not interested in the program that I had going with IP's John Perry. John was a forester for IP until they sold out here. Over the years we've remained in touch and good friends. He was very nice to deal with.

Lou Dunyon from Utah is happy.

Author and his Oregon muzzlelader whitetail from northeastern Oregon.

Chapter Eighteen

OREGON SUPER SLAM

While sheep hunting with Elvin Hawkins on Hart mountain in '88 I asked him if he knew of anyone in the state that had killed one of each of the nine species of game in Oregon. Elvin knew almost all of the sheep hunters in the state at that time and if he didn't know them personally, he'd call them after their hunt to see how they had done. He was connected! He thought awhile and then said that, "No, he did not know of any successful sheep hunters that had also killed both Roosevelt's elk and Rocky Mountain elk plus mule deer, whitetail deer, blacktail deer, cougar, black bear and antelope. I told him of my plan to be the first as I couldn't think of anyone I knew of that had done it either. About this time I was in the middle of a two-year stint of writing a column for the *Oregon Hunter* Magazine, so I inquired there as to whether or not anyone had knowledge of anyone taking all nine species. No replies! The sheep tags were the hardest obstacle to overcome, but very few had killed a whitetail in Oregon and many hunters had not killed a Roosevelt elk because so many only hunted the elk in eastern Oregon. Well, I had my Oregon ram now, but I still needed the whitetail and the cougar. I'd killed a cougar in northeastern Washington a few years earlier and had taken a nice Oregon buck antelope in '79.

The following year I applied for a whitetail, muzzleloader tag and a cougar tag. I drew the deer tag, but failed to fill it due to several reasons, one being lack of experience and another being pre-focused on serious problems at work. The next year I applied for both again, but changed deer areas. I was not used to hunting whitetails so I called a fellow in northeastern Oregon that I knew. Galen Clark not only knew where to go and how to hunt them, but invited me to park my camper in his yard and go with him. I jumped at the chance as I knew he had taken some nice

From left are author and Mike Shirley after Duane completed fulfilling the Oregon Super Slam.

whiteys with his muzzleloader. I had one great advantage when hunting with Galen; he had permission to hunt on about half of the farms near his home in Elgin. I'm not knocking his method because it worked, but his approach to hunting whitetail in this late season with black powder was unheard of to me. Galen was in no hurry to be out at first light as I'm used to. We drank coffee until the school bus passed his house and then we left the driveway, and FOLLOWED the bus. When the bus would stop, which was very often, Galen would bring up his binocular to glass around the barns, corrals and fence rows for deer. I learned something from him. He had permission to hunt most of the land and if he didn't he knew who to go see to get it. Seemed like we'd stop about every quarter of a mile and glass 'til the bus started out again. It worked because we spotted a group of deer, parked his truck, made a lengthy stalk and I killed a nice 4x5 point, plus eye guards that made the black powder record book. The next day Galen got his buck about the same way.

Now I only lacked one animal to complete the Oregon Super Slam and I had a tag for cougar in my pocket. Friend Mike Rahn in Enterprise had recommended a friend of his in Wallowa by the name of Mike Shirley, who owned some good cat hounds. I soon struck a deal with

Mike putting the dogs away on the author's truck

Mike where I used my Dodge diesel truck and he furnished only the dogs. I stayed in Enterprise with Mike Rahn and his wife. I was out early the next morning to pick up Mike Shirley and luck was with us as we had about three inches of new snow. I'd told Mike that I wanted about two feet of snow, but only about two to three inches each day. Within an hour I saw a fresh track on my side of the truck and when Mike confirmed it, he turned all the dogs loose and the race was on. The big cat actually crossed the highway, but treed soon after. When we got there the cat was sitting about 16 feet up and out on the end of a limb. Afraid he'd jump, I hurriedly put a .50 caliber ball into his chest and heart. Before noon on December 3rd, 1990, I had fulfilled my goal. I had my nine Oregon big game animals and as far as I know I was the first to ever do so. This was later acknowledged by the people from the Oregon Record Book at a reception in Portland. The Oregon Hunters Association made mention of it too. Shortly after that someone decided they should add turkeys and make it ten species. Next it became legal to hunt mountain goats in Oregon if you drew a permit, so now there are eleven species in the slam.

Besides the original nine, I have turkey, so now I hope and pray for a goat tag in Oregon before I'm too old to shoot one. Regardless, I've got my Oregon Super Slam and I'm proud of it. I also have a daughter-in-law who is lacking few animals for the slam but she has the hard-to-get ones too; sheep, antelope,cougar and bear.

Chapter Nineteen

MONTANA

In November of '92 when the hunting on the lease was coming to a close in Oregon, I left for a mule deer and whitetail hunt that I had booked in southeast British Columbia. I planned to go over into the Bitterroot Valley of Montana to visit my longtime friend, Olin Curtis, who had recently moved there with his wife, Merle. Ole was a brother to Bill Curtis that you read about earlier in this book of happenings and encounters. I had a couple of days to visit Ole and Merle before I had to leave for my hunt in Canada. I'd always liked the area there ever since I'd packed into the Selway-Bitterroot Wilderness from the Montana side. Ole told me about several pieces of land that were for sale, but after looking at them I passed on them, but I did decide to call a realtor to see what was available. To make a long story short, I bought a place in the valley, not too far from Ole, but yet very handy to hunting, fishing, four-wheeling, hiking and snowmobiling. Hard to beat all that! I called Joanne and told her before I went on to Canada for the hunt. This little chunk of land even had a nice creek running through it. Not much flat ground, but enough for what we'd use it for. It was the next spring before Joanne got to see it.

When we were able to get back over there in the spring of '93 we put in a driveway, cut and burned brush and dug a shallow well in the yard. Ole and Merle lived close enough to spend a lot of time up there with us, either just visiting or four-wheeling with us. They liked to ride along slowly on the four-wheelers and look at all the game. The amount of game there and the variety of game is what made me decide to purchase land there. We could always see elk, mule deer, whitetail deer and moose. Occasionally we'd see bear and bighorn sheep and of course there were always cougar, but lately the wolf seems to be the dominant predator. We soon started to work on a small log cabin and with the help of friends and family we nearly completed it by the end of summer in '94. In August of that year, Joanne and I were accompanied by Dale Trautman, Les Mortenson and Steve Chambers as we hauled a load of tools and equipment and some furnishings to Montana. I'd scheduled a load of logs that had slabs off of two sides (top & bottom) to be delivered the next day. As work progressed more people showed up to help as some had to leave to go home. At one time I think Joanne was cooking for 17 people including a few grandkids. All four of our kids showed up with their families at different times so we didn't have too many there at once. When it would get too hot in the afternoon to work (Dale called it "beer time") Joanne and I would go to town to buy more materials and supplies while the "crew" would go four-wheeling or swimming. Two weeks later we were able move some furnishings inside and close the door to go home to Oregon. It wasn't all done inside, but close enough for that year.

The next spring Joanne and I took over cabinets, a wood stove and a pre-fabbed outhouse. Ole and Merle, as well as Steve Chambers were frequent guests that summer. It was common to have large groups in the

Cabin building in Montana.

Four-wheeling in Montana with our little dog, Penny.

yard in the evenings as we cooked, ate and listened to Ole's tales about his younger days in northern Alberta, Canada. He was a good story-teller and some of these were quite funny. Examples: his spring moose hunts, his trapline experiences, muskrat hunting with a .22, etc., etc., etc. He always had an interesting story to tell. Ole also had a funny little saying that was a holdover from his days on the trapline: "hitch up the dogs, piss on the fire and let's hit the trail". He liked our little cabin and Jo and I will always miss him.

In the summer of '98 a neighbor showed his stupidity by burning trash in his yard which resulted in a sudden forest fire that swept through the forest above our cabin; it burned about 5,500 acres in the area.. We were not there at the time, but it came within about 80 yards of the cabin. We lost most of the trees on the place. Two years later, in the summer of 2000, Montana saw their worst forest fire season ever in the southwestern part of the state. We were not so lucky that year – we lost it all. We were at home in Oregon, but Ole kept us up to date on things there and when the fire was getting too close for our comfort, our good friend, Ken Nagle from Vancouver, Washington, joined me about 2:00 a.m. one morning. We headed to Montana to haul back what we could in case the fire got the cabin. I had my four-wheeler and an enclosed utility trailer parked in the yard there, plus all of the stuff in the cabin. When Ken and I approached the guard at the end of the road he informed us that we were lucky as the wind had switched and the Forest Service thought our place would be spared. With that new information we decided to only take the four-wheeler and the trailer, along with my saddle and Ole's old snowshoes with the lamp wick binding, and start back to Oregon. While inside Ken picked up Joanne's photo album and asked, "What about this"? I told him to leave it as we'd just have to bring it back later. Little did I know that I'd never see that beautiful little cabin again! The day after we got back home I received word from Ole that our cabin had burned completely, along with 18 others in that neighborhood, on August 6th, 2000.

I had been involved with, and on the board of directors of the Portland Chapter of Safari Club since its inception. I went on to become president of that fine group and consequently was on the board of directors for the parent organization, Safari Club International based in Tucson, Arizona. I was on my way back from a board of directors meeting in Jackson, Wyoming, in early September when I decided to drive by to see what it looked like. How sad that sight was! All the hard work, memories, fun times, family antiques, Joanne's photo album, plus

Jo takes a break at our newly-built and nearly-finished cabin.

the cabin itself were gone. Devastating ! Everything in sight was black. All the trees that were left, the ground, the concrete – everything was all black.

Joanne and I went back over soon after and cleaned it all up, hauling the junk to the dump. We were one of the first to do so. I felt like we were burying an old friend that had died prematurely.

Well, by the following spring we had another one started in its place. We hired this one built though. I didn't have the heart to ask the family and friends to do that work again and I knew I was getting too old to do it anyway. Joanne likes the new one better. It's okay, but we did a better job on the original one.

One day's hunting. From left are Steve Chambers, Bill Harrel and the author.

The 2001 fire about a mile from the cabin.

This is what our cabin looked like after the fire.

Chapter Twenty

STEEN'S MOUNTAIN EXPERIENCE

I think it was the fall of '95 when I drew a mule deer tag to hunt on Oregon's Steen's Mountain. This area was some of the best in Oregon at one time, but that was long before 1995. For those that may know it, the Steen's Mountain is a very rough country and home to mule deer, California bighorns, elk and cougar – with antelope scattered around the base of the mountain.

This was to be a solo trip for me, which I don't mind at all. I didn't have any great expectations of getting a big buck there, but was looking forward to getting away. I started out the season up on top in fog and eight to ten inches of snow. The snow was melting fast and I spent a couple of days hunting from my camper up there without seeing one decent deer. I broke camp and drove down and around to the southeast base of the mountain, where I put on my backpack and tried hiking up away from the gravel road. This didn't improve the deer hunting any but I did have a couple of interesting experiences there, besides getting to spot a cougar while glassing for bucks. While hunting in a new part of the area there one day I came upon an Indian "medicine tree". The only other one I'd ever seen or knew of was in the Bitterroot Valley of Montana. But make no mistake about it, here was one in Oregon too. Not very handy to a road either, but it was decorated very similar to the one in Montana. Maybe someone knows why the Indians decorate certain trees to this extent, but I sure don't and I've never been able to find out much about medicine trees. A few years later I was able to show it to other members of the family and to some friends. The next day, I believe it was, I had a very scary thing happen to me that is both hard to explain and hard to believe. I was hunting across a very big broad flat towards a deep and steep canyon that I wanted to approach unnoticed and glass into. I did NOT want to just walk up to the edge and start glassing because that would be apt to spook deer if there were any in the deep hole. So, as I got to where I could see some of the area just under the rimrock on the far side I stopped and glassed it before moving up a few feet and glassing the next segment lower down on the far side. I planned on doing this until I could see the very bottom of the canyon in order to avoid spooking any deer that may be there. As stated, I was on a big flat plateau and at least 35 feet back from the edge, so I was not paying too much attention to where I was stepping. Then I happened to look down by my feet and I could see green sagebrush way, way down beneath me! Talk about a scare!!! I very suddenly fell back onto the ground behind me and tried to collect my wits. I do NOT like high places, especially when they're not too safe and I'm alone. When I got to my feet and regained composure I discovered that apparently the ground in front of me was under-mined, and I was actually getting ready to step out onto the overhang that had partially fractured from the surrounding earth. I could now look straight down between my feet and again see sagebrush. How scary! I took a couple of pictures of it as best I could and was glad to leave. It may have been hanging there in that position for centuries and

Picture taken looking straight down at my feet. See the sagebrush through the hole in the ground.

it may continue for many more, but I sure didn't like it at all. Can you imagine being there during an earthquake?

The next day when I was back at my camper, my old buddy, Steve Chambers, showed up. Steve lives in Kelso, Washington, and he couldn't hunt where I was, but wanted to come check on me I guess. I soon told Steve of the large crack in the ground and the scare it had given me. The next day, I took him up to see it for himself. On the way up there we even stopped by the medicine tree. That night we soaked in the Alvord Hot Springs, a much needed bath for me.

From left are Steve Chambers, professional hunter Jonnie Johnson and tracker Chulinga with Steve's large lion

Chapter Twenty-one

ZIMBABWE SAFARI

When the fall of '94 rolled around I was ready to go back to Africa. Jo is always ready to go. I had persuaded Steve Chambers to accompany us, along with our daughter, Carma, and her husband, Bill Harrel. Steve, on his first trip to Africa, would be hunting lion, buffalo and plains game. I wanted a leopard, buffalo and a large kudu mainly. Carma and Bill would hunt plains game only. Joanne was not hunting this time. I'd booked the fourteen-day hunt with Hippo Valley Safaris out of Chiredzi, Zimbabwe, to commence on September 26th, so we left Portland International Airport on Joanne's birthday (Sept. 22nd) headed for London. From there we flew straight through to Harare, Zimbabwe. We had a day and a half there to shop and see the city before we were scheduled to take the six and a half hour van ride to Chiredzi.

Our professional hunter, Gary Baldwin, met us there and took us the remaining 45 minute ride to a very wonderful safari camp. We ate a great and late dinner and crashed for the night. Joanne and I had our own chalet, as did Carma and Bill. Steve had his as well.

The next morning after checking our rifles, Gary informed me that he'd been baiting a large male leopard for several days. He suggested we go have a look to see if the cat was still coming in to the bait. I was to hunt with Gary and his trackers, Shumba and Jimmy, while Steve would be hunting with Professional Hunter Jonnie Johnson and their trackers, Chulinga and John. Carma and Bill would have a young lad by the name of Griffen to help them.

When Gary, I, Joanne and the trackers arrived at the bait station it was evident that the leopard was still patronizing the place. They built a blind exactly 50 yards from the bait tree. I had been shooting my custom .375 H&H magnum at that distance and was able to regularly hit bottle caps with it and the 1¾-6 Leupold scope that is on it. Things were looking good when we left to take Jo back to camp and get some lunch while we waited to start the afternoon trip back to the blind.

That afternoon as we cautiously approached the blind and the trackers drove off about a half mile, my mind was racing in anticipation of this new type of hunting for a species that I very much desired. Gary and I settled into the chairs and he quietly instructed me about the signals he'd use to alert me when the leopard approached and also when to get ready to shoot and finally when to shoot. We'd not ever whisper a word, only communicate by motions! We were to sit perfectly still. Because I'm hard of hearing, I'd elected to wear my "Action Ears" – sound amplifiers that fit over your head like ear muffs. I turned them on and was able to hear all of the interesting "jungle" sounds. All the birds and animals were busy, it seemed, filling up before dark. It was really quite noisy. Gary had warned me that when the cat came in everything would suddenly become quiet as the smaller birds and animals would decide it prudent to keep a low profile. After about an hour that is exactly what happened. An impala somewhere gave a warning bark and then all was quiet. About five tense minutes later, with my hearing enhancement, I could hear the leopard walking behind our blind. How far away, I do not know, but I'd guess about eight to ten feet. Talk about a rush! It sounded to me like he walked from the blind down into a dry wash that led to the bait tree. The next thing I heard was him tearing at the bait. Gary signaled to get ready.

The bait was actually suspended from a leaning tree and was up off the ground about three to four feet. When I first saw him, he was standing on his hind feet with his front feet trying to hold the swinging bait still. Gary had already instructed me to not shoot 'til I had a broadside shot. In the excitement, I guess I forgot that, or just call it "hunter's intuition" but when he was still in that position I had my .375 H&H trained on a rosette between his shoulder blades as his back was towards me. I squeezed the trigger! The cat ran off. Gary was visibly upset with me. "Why didn't you wait like I told you" he asked? I explained that the shot felt good, but that hardly justified anything as the leopard was nowhere in sight. Soon the trackers, Jimmy and Shumba, showed up. Gary had grabbed his shotgun loaded with buckshot. We held a council of war and Gary explained that this may not be fun as he thought the cat was wounded and it was now getting quite dark. We went slowly to the bait tree and found evidence of a hit. The next 100 yards continued to show more blood, but no cat. (At least, there was no cat attack either.) Finally the blood trail led to a mound of green vegetation that was really quite open underneath due to warthogs, etc. spending much time under there. Gary, with shotgun in hand, knelt and shined the light under the brush and could see some spots, but couldn't tell which way the cat laid or if it was dead or alive. After several small sticks and rocks were thrown it was determined to be very dead, but I would not have wanted to have been the tracker that had to crawl in there and drag it out. Then we celebrated, took pictures and I could relax at last. It had been a very stressful evening, but I knew I had been very lucky to get my leopard the first night.

After we'd gotten him out to the Landcruiser and drove the 40 miles or so back to the camp, it was quite late and I had to wake the rest of the party to come see my leopard. I knew now that I had picked a very good PH. I found out also that Steve had killed a zebra that day.

The following day Steve got his kudu and the next day got a warthog and an eland. Meanwhile, I was having trouble finding a good kudu. On Saturday, October first, Steve got a very large lion, I got a 53" kudu, Carma shot an impala and Bill killed a bush pig. Carma was able to get

Author with his 53-inch kudu bull.

On October 3rd Jonnie was able to get Steve into a small herd of cape buffalo, TWICE. The first time Steve missed the biggest bull of the bunch, but the second time was the charm here as Steve got a very nice buffalo. Steve was having the time of his life and never once regretted being "talked into going". Meanwhile, on that day I found a very nice waterbuck to take home to our den. The following day Steve and Carma each killed bushbucks.

On October 5th Gary Baldwin, myself and the trackers managed to get into the same bunch of cape buffalo that Steve had taken his from two days before. All morning long when we'd get close to them the swirling wind would give us away. Finally about noon Gary suggested that we go find the Landcruiser, eat lunch and come back in the afternoon when the wind should be more consistent. After lunch we had no trouble finding the herd of 30 to 35 animals and Gary was right, the wind had died down. We sneaked in close (about 50 yards) at about 12:30 and remained in that proximity to the herd 'til about 4:30 when the biggest bull of the bunch decided to stand up and offer me a good shot. We were sitting on the

Author with his Cape Buffalo bull and his .375 H&H magnum.

ground and I was using my shooting sticks that Shumba had made for me. I took one shot at his shoulder when he was broadside and he ran in a tight lefthand circle while the others all vacated the area, thankfully. When he stopped in nearly the same spot, I shot again and that put him down. That wonderful death bellow followed soon thereafter.

It was late in the day so while Gary and I rested and took pictures, he sent Shumba for the Landcruiser while Jimmy was instructed to go round up some help to load this huge critter. He would try to catch some of the local cane cutters as they walked home from a day in the fields. They both arrived back about the same time. Jimmy had been told to get three to four fellows; he came with six or seven. They all wanted some of the bull. This turned out to be one of the best trades I'd ever witnessed. They butchered the bull (went at it like they were killing snakes), loaded him in the Landcruiser and then each took an armful of the guts and headed merrily down the trail towards home. There is definitely a protein shortage there.

Curiously, this bull had an old bullet hole in his left ear, about .375 size. Someone had shot at him before. Long before! I knew that Steve had shot at him two days before too. After he was all loaded up, I daubed

Daughter Carma and tracker with her Impala ram.

my finger in some fresh blood and then poked my finger into the old bullet hole in his ear. Upon arrival at the skinning shed Steve was waiting for us as we'd radioed ahead and told them of our luck. He congratulated me and then when he saw the bull he said "yeah that's the one I missed". I corrected him. "Steve you didn't miss". When hunting in Africa the rule is that if you hit or wound an animal you must pay the trophy fee anyway. I reminded Steve of this and told him he may have to pay the trophy fee on my bull. He was shocked and asked where he'd hit it. By this time his PH, Jonnie, was there too and was very concerned because he'd told Steve that he missed the bull. They both asked where he'd hit it and when I showed them the hole in the ear they were both dumbfounded. Steve said "How in the hell did I hit him there"? I could not keep from laughing any longer. Then I wiped away the blood and showed them the old hole. That hole is still there and I still chuckle when I see it.

Steve took a duiker the next day and Bill took a duiker and a warthog.

Bill shot an impala the following day and that evening I shot a genet cat after dark with a shotgun and using Gary's dog, Bonsie, a Jack

Our group and our trophies.

Russell terrier. Next day I got a baboon and Bill shot a zebra.

We were then treated to a trip to Chulinga's village where some of his wives lived while one or two were at camp with him when he was there. This was all very interesting. The chief was Chulinga's uncle and in order to be admitted into the village we had to take him an impala. After inquiring at his home, we found the chief drinking beer with the boys. His wives each had there own hut in a semi-circle around a little tool hut that was community property for any of them to use. Nice of him to let any and all of them use his axes, scythes, hoes, buckets, churns, hammers and etc. Right? It was his choice as to where he spent the nights. We also saw where the village court was held. Just a few homemade wooden benches and a home-made lectern in front

This was one of our best trips ever, with good professionals, good friends and family, lots of game and a beautiful safari camp. Although this is primarily a sugar cane plantation, it also has excellent game animals. It is huge. The town of Chiredzi is built on the old original plantation. Over seven thousand people are employed there in the cane fields. We'll never forget Gary and this hunt. I'm sure that Bill, Carma and Steve will all someday return to Africa.

Jerry's base camp at Tucho Lake upon our arrival.

Chapter Twenty-two

ROLLING STONE RAMS

My 30-something son, Dave, isn't a horseman, but he was doing quite well during the first leg of our horseback ride into camp. It was August of '97 and we were in northern British Columbia on a Stone sheep hunt with Upper Stikine Outfitters and my longtime friend, Jerry Geraci. Though this area is mountainous, and can be treacherous, our mounts were familiar with the terrain. Stone sheep are a hearty, high altitude species, and it would take some work to reach them.

By midday we entered a large picturesque valley wrapped with green meadows, wildflowers and streams. The valley was surrounded by snowy forested mountains against an azure backdrop of a sweeping, breath taking view. It was also an ideal spot to set up the main horse camp. A group of wranglers would stay with the 20 horses while Dave and I and our guides Jerry and Glen would backpack into higher country to set up a spike camp for the fourteen-day sheep hunt.

We rose early for the hike which wasn't as difficult as we had expected. Reaching a spot above timberline we set up camp at a spot that Jerry had used before. Not only was there a large flat boulder that functioned as a table, but a small mountain stream also burbled nearby giving us a convenient water source. When the sky was clear the view was breathtaking.

After arranging camp, Dave, Jerry and I decided to take a short hike around a mountain pass to look for sheep sign. Although the sheep were not visible we knew we were in the right place.

As the sun settled beyond the westward reaching mountain ranges we returned to camp, ate some supper and crawled into our sleeping bags. Dave and I were sharing one small tent while Jerry and Glen shared another. Sleep came easy for both Dave and I as we were looking forward to starting the hunt. After so much planning and preparation we actually were here and tomorrow we'd be trying to locate a couple of rams. But come the first light of dawn, would we ever be in for a surprise!

Ten years ago I had unsuccessfully pursued these wily sheep. Now retired, I hoped to cheat fate and take one home with me. This time Dave would be joining me. I only hoped he would enjoy these Canadian mountains as much as I did. Now that I was in my 60's I also wondered if this would be my last sheep hunt.

We left our homes in northwest Oregon and enjoyed a leisurely drive north to Smithers , B.C., where we were met by our friend, Jerry Geraci. We pulled into Jerry's yard late in the day and were invited in for dinner. We also accepted his invitation to spend the night there too as we'd all be leaving early the next morning for Tattoga Lake. Once there we'd meet Murry Woods for the charter flight in the Cassiar Mountains. Dave and I were Jerry's first hunters of the season so he'd be flying in with us. Other guide, wranglers, cooks and assorted help had already trailed 35 horses approximately 200 miles cross country to Tucho Lake, where we planned to meet them.

The 100-mile flight over the mountain wilderness was spectacular. We saw goats and moose and were dazzled by the scenery. Murry, a seasoned pilot, had just celebrated fifty years of safe piloting and was honored at a party hosted by the local guides and outfitters.

Tucho Lake, ringed by tall mountain peaks, was just as pretty and inviting as ever. To me it was like coming home: the sky blue waters, corrals full of husky pack and saddle horses, a twelve-foot aluminum fishing boat beside the dock and wisps of smoke curling from the chimney of the main log cabin all promised leisure and tranquility. Dave was awestruck by its beauty. The pictures that his mother and I had shown him just didn't do it justice.

After we helped unload the plane we were introduced to the cook, Izzy, the wrangler, Don, and Dave's guide, Glen Holmes. We just got our gear stored in the cabin when Izzy called us for lunch. A nap could wait.

In the morning Dave and I started sorting through our gear trying to decide what to leave at base camp and what to take along for the pack trip into sheep country. Meanwhile Jerry, Glen, Don and Don's apprentice, Dusty, were saddling horses, making up packs. The ride to our horse camp would take seven hours, but thanks to the new saddles that Jerry had made in Montana, the ride actually was comfortable.

As daylight began to beat back the darkness on what would be our first day of hunting from spike camp we were awakened by the sound of rolling rocks and boulders. But this didn't sound like a few small rocks plinking down the cliffs! It sounded like a lot of rocks falling down the mountainside toward our tents.

"What the hell?" I said aloud as Dave and I quickly scrambled out of our sleeping bags and fumbled with the tent zippers. We nearly tore the tent in two trying to get out and once we did, we were shocked – and only half dressed. In total defiance of gravity a Stone ram was standing about 100 yards away on the very steep mountainside. It was as if the sub-adult male knew that its three-quarter curl horns protected it from being one of our trophies, and it was simply teasing us.

This was not the first sheep hunt for either of us. I'd taken three other sheep and had hunted once before with Jerry Geraci, although I didn't get my ram. Dave was an experienced sheep guide and had certainly seen enough sheep to know as I did that this wasn't the way things usually started.

Well, where were our sheep guides? We had rifles and rams but no pants or guides. A soft call to the other tent brought out Jerry and Glen,

Author with son, Dave, with their rams.

like us, not completely dressed.

As we all hunkered down behind our boulder/table trying to look inconspicuous, someone spotted a couple more rams in the pass above us, slowly coming our way. One of them was a very large ram, but too far away to shoot and to close for us to maneuver away from camp and intercept them without being seen. When they dropped into a shallow ravine out of sight the ram above us moved out also.

We dressed quickly and Dave, Jerry and I started up the mountain to see if we could spot them again or at least see which way they went. Glen stayed in camp to continue watching. A wise decision as it turned out, as he saw them again and we did not. We soon returned to camp. Coffee was long overdue. What an exciting way to start a sheep hunt!

After some coffee and snacks we all set off again to try to gain enough altitude to be able to see the rams again. By making a big, circuitous climb above the pass we were able to get in a good position to glass. It didn't take long to pick out seven rams grazing in the middle of a grassy slope below us – and on the opposite side of the pass above our spike camp. We dropped over the back side of the ridge from which we were glassing and swung back into the pass above our camp. We expected to be able to see the rams again if they hadn't moved too far. It required some tricky maneuvering on our part because the ridge was covered with loose boulders. We still had our packs on too, which didn't help.

As soon as we got into the pass we spotted the sheep near the far side of the grassy slope. We watched as they slowly fed up the hillside. When they fed over the top and out of sight, Jerry nodded and we charged after them. As we approached the top of the hill we slowed down and moved more cautiously. We knelt behind some large rocks and peeked over, immediately spotting the largest of the seven rams.

As we came through the pass earlier we had seen another group of three rams farther off. That made ten rams in the area and the largest was only about 100 yards in front of us. Day one was looking good.

I was beginning to realize that at 60 years of age, I was about 30 years older than I had been at 50 when I'd last hunted here, so shooting the ram on the first day was OK with me. In fact it was fine. After watching it for a few minutes it was time to put my tag on him. One shot from my left-handed 7mm Remington magnum and the sheep was mine. Then Dave had to decide which of the other two rams he wanted, if either. As the sheep started trotting away, above us, on the mountainside

Our spike camp with "meat on the table."

my son fired one shot and had his Stone ram.

Two hunters, two shots and two fine rams only 150 yards apart. Things weren't looking too shabby! My ram was nearly eleven years old and had wide-flaring, 38-inch horns that still had both lamb tips. Dave's ram was about ten years old with a beautiful set of horns and a nice dark cape.

We spent the rest of our time fishing, visiting in camp and sightseeing from horseback.

When Murry and the Beaver came in on schedule at the end of our allotted time, Dave was eager to start home. For me, however, it was a sad farewell to good friends and a special little spot in the Cassiars that I probably will never get the chance to see again.

At least this time fate had been my friend. This was my fourth ram, and in all honesty, I reckon it will be my last.

From left are Joanne, Jerry and Duane on the author's first Stone sheep hunt, at Tucho Lake.

Chapter Twenty-three

SOUTHERN OREGON BLACKTAILS

In the fall of '97 I had drawn a muzzleloader tag for blacktail in southern Oregon. Considering that Dave and I had just returned from a grueling Stone sheep hunt in British Columbia, hunting blacktails in my home state of Oregon should have been a relatively easy feat – or at least not too strenuous. Right? Fat chance! As I soon discovered, these are wily deer, quite able to give hunters the run around in the Pacific Northwest.

I enjoy hunting alone, I like to use a muzzleloader and I always enjoy hunting big bucks. I was eagerly anticipating my hunt for Columbia blacktails in Oregon. I had been lucky in the drawing and would now get to participate in the muzzleloader season – the only hunt in the November rut. The fact that this area would be new to me provided an additional challenge.

After days of scouting and studying maps it was time to leave my home in northwest Oregon. I arrived two days early to allow myself more scouting time, but was met with pea-soup fog that lasted both days. The fog was so thick that the visibility was cut to a fifty-yard maximum. So much for glassing and trying to learn the country!

Opening day dawned with about half the area still in fog, but this was an improvement. I could at least attempt to do some hunting.

I saw deer each day and was learning the area but I decided to hold out for a nice buck or go home empty-handed. I was hunting the steep canyons a mile or so from my camp. To be there at dawn required getting up early. On most days I stayed until dark, then hiked out for supper. Afterward I'd fix my lunch for the next day and crawl into my sleeping bag.

I continued seeing small bucks until the seventh day when I located a 4x4 blacktail buck and several does about a half a mile away in the bottom of a canyon. I mentally mapped out a map to it and took off. By the time I got there the buck and his does had retreated into the heavy brush.

The eighth day brought heavy rain and only mediocre bucks. One thing I was noticing, and to my pleasure, was the lack of hunters this far from the road.

On the ninth I glassed a huge blacktail buck in still another canyon about half a mile away. I shed my pack and taking only a water bottle, sandwich and a flashlight I started out after it. I think I made a good stalk but the buck was not to be found when I got there. I was in the bottom of the canyon and knew that there was at least one good buck in the area so I decided to spend the day sitting here watching and waiting 'til dark if necessary. Unfortunately, all I saw was a couple of does right at twilight just as I prepared to start my climb out by flashlight. It had not been a very exciting day.

Although the rut seemed to be warming up each day, this routine was starting to wear down this 60-year-old deer hunter, regardless of having

Another book blacktail taken with the muzzleloader. Notice the old shooting sticks.

The author's best black powder blacktail buck.

been in "sheep shape" earlier in the fall. These canyons were steep and far from camp. Though I'd made plans to hunt the entire three week season if I had to, I was beginning to hope it wouldn't take that long to find the buck I wanted.

The morning of the tenth day found me again about a mile and a half from camp as it started to get light. Right away I spotted several deer crossing a small meadow, heading to a thick patch of brush. By going slow, keeping low and using what little bit of cover was available to me I was able to get about 75 yards farther down the hill and on a collision course with the deer. I was unaware that the 4x4 buck I'd tried to reach the day before was with this small group of does.

I ran out of cover just as it was getting light enough to shoot, and as I sat hunkered down in very little brush and tall grass, the buck stopped broadside about 125 yard away. It had no idea that anyone was in that canyon. After nine days it was now all coming together just right. One shot from my .50 caliber muzzleloader and the hunt was over.

After several trips out with meat, horns and cape, I was finally able to sit down, relax and admire my trophy.

It takes 105 points for a Columbian blacktail to make the SCI record book and this beautiful buck scored 135 6/8 points, 24 1/8 points more than the No. 1 muzzleloader-taken buck in the Record Book's Edition IX.

Persistence had definitely paid off for this old deer hunter, and if I wasn't in shape after sheep hunting I sure was now.

Two years later in '99 I drew another muzzleloader tag for that area and, hunting solo again, shot a very nice, wide 3x3 buck. That one came from a different place though; a place I call "buck point".

Chapter Twenty-four

THE SHEEP HUNT FROM HELL

Following the family trend, son Dave drew an Oregon sheep tag in '98. He already knew he would be joined by several of his hunting buddies, but nonetheless asked his mother and I to join him also. His twin brother, Dan, and Dan's wife would go also to help scout, pack or whatever. The tag was for an area near Steen's Mountain. Dale Trautman and I had planned a backpack deer hunt in western Wyoming right after this sheep hunt, so Dale joined us also on the sheep hunt. Dale and I planned to go on to Wyoming from there and Joanne would come home with the kids. We had a large group! All of us except Dave's hunting buddies left from our home while they had left earlier. We had planned to caravan the four vehicles from here that morning.

While towing his travel trailer through Portland, Dan was following another car a little too close and had a "fender bender". Slowed us down some but no big deal! We'd still caravan to camp. Then, on the east side of the Cascade Mountains, Dale blew a trailer tire. He had the trailer loaded quite heavy with a four-wheeler, various tools and equipment and a couple of extra propane tanks. I stopped to help Dale while the other two rigs proceeded to the next wide spot to wait for us. We were all in radio contact as we tried to travel together. Dale and I soon had his spare trailer tire on and caught up with Dave and Dan and their wives. We soon found out that Dave's problems were a little more serious than the previous ones for the day. The transmission in his Ford pickup was about on its last leg. Joanne and I were hauling our camper on our Dodge diesel pickup. We were the only ones with out a trailer behind. It was decided that we should pull Dave and Renay's travel trailer to lighten the load on their sick rig. We'd also transfer all the heavy stuff, like beer, canned food, beer, soda pop, beer, gas and beer into Dave's trailer, behind my

Dodge while Dave tried to get his Ford to a garage in Madras, Oregon.

We drove slow and Dave made it to Madras okay. After leaving instructions with the mechanic on duty, Dave told him he'd return for his Ford after he filled his sheep tag. We were off again with Dave and Renay riding with Dale in his Dodge.

Everything seemed to be going fine, but it was taking us a long time to make the seven hour drive to camp with all these delays. As we approached the anticipated camp site, I, being in the lead, slowed to make the turn across the barrow pit along the road. I made a very slow turn with Dave's trailer behind me. When I'd gotten across I stopped to get out and go back to ask them where they wanted to park. What a heck of a sight! Theirs was a tandem axle trailer but now there was only a single axle on the lefthand side when I got out. I discovered the other wheel and tire behind the trailer, at a right angle to where it should have been. The axle was badly bent and sticking out behind the trailer. The holding tank had been broken when the axle assumed its odd position. Some spring shackles and "U" bolts were bent and some were missing altogether. What a mess!

Apparently some of the cattle guards that I'd crossed, I'd taken just

Dave's trailer at arrival in our camp.

a little too fast. I failed to take into consideration the fact that their trailer was loaded so heavy with all that beverage, etc. Then, when I'd crossed the barrow pit, the left end of the axle pivoted around to the rear of the trailer. Boy did I feel terrible! A couple of those cattle guards were extremely rough and with no warning, except the standard sign. Not being used to the road we didn't know they were so rough.

Well Dave did get his ram. A very nice one too. Then we tore into the trailer as we still had a long drive home. We wedged the axle into the fork of a big juniper tree and I hooked on to it with my winch cable and straightened it somewhat. But not enough! The owner of the little store and station in Fields was very sympathetic and very generous. He opened up his shop to us and just told us to use what we needed. A little heat on that cold steel sure made a difference. A little pounding and prying and it looked "trail worthy".

Now that the work and the hunting were done I took the group up to show them the "Indian Tree" that I'd found a few years before and had shown to Steve Chambers. Next we paid a visit to the Alvord Hot Springs for some much needed relaxing and bathing.

They took it slow all the way home, due to the trailer, but made it fine. They stopped in Madras to pick up Dave's Ford as it was done and in good shape.

Dale I had meanwhile headed to Wyoming for our backpack mule deer hunt.

Right where he fell. The best hunt of my life.

Chapter Twenty-five

MY BIG MONTANA MULEY

Like many other deer hunters, I'd been searching, hunting, scouting, hoping and praying for a large buck mule deer to put on my wall. This was a quest that continued approximately forty years. My search has led me to all the western states except California and I've hunted some states quite a few times. I love Idaho and their deer hunting, both whitetails and muleys. In this search for a large mule deer buck, I've hunted on both public and private land, hunted early and late seasons, hunted with and without guides and used horses, four-wheelers, tents, motor homes and what ever I thought it would take to get the job done. I've always been fairly lucky in the "draw" but I'm not a lucky hunter. I must work hard for what I get. Not complaining, just stating the facts! My desire to kill a large mule deer has led me to some very good areas, but for one reason or another I always came back home just a little dissatisfied, even when I managed to kill a fairly decent buck. Maybe I failed to hold off long enough. Sometimes of course the weather was all wrong. Some of the guided hunts were a disappointment because after booking the hunt a year or so in advance it always seemed like the weather would end up being warm and mild when I'd planned for cold and snow. I've hunted Utah's Deseret Ranch, New Mexico's Jicarilla Indian Reservation, the Gila National Forest, British Columbia and Alberta, Canada, with no real satisfaction and nice bucks – but not nice enough to satisfy. Many hunters will say, and I agree, that to get a mule deer into the record books is the hardest of all species hunted in North America.

As I stated in an earlier chapter, one of the deciding factors in us buying our place in Montana was the large amount of game animals there and also the large variety of game. I suppose there is better mule deer country, but because I know the area there so well and see these bucks three seasons out of the four in the year I always felt that I had a good chance of getting a real nice buck IF I could just get drawn there. Many is the time that I've told Joanne that I'd give almost anything to just have a mule deer tag there. Once I even made the mistake of telling her how much I'd be willing to pay for one if you could just go to town and purchase it. That was a mistake. She never talked to me for a couple of days.

As stated earlier, the forest fires in that region in the year 2000 were devastating. As you may know though, a forest fire actually is good for the game in the long run. The animals rebound unbelievably fast. Such was the case in Montana after those fires.

In the mid-nineties much of the mule deer's winter range in this part of Montana was rapidly fenced off for commercial elk ranching. That means twelve-foot fences with an electric wire also, thus making it very hard on deer as well as the wild elk. The Montana Department of Fish, Wildlife and Parks countered by practically eliminating the buck mule deer hunting here and limiting it to only 25 tags for buck mule deer. They've increased the total now somewhat, but a tag there is still very hard to come by.

Then in late August of '03, I got the surprise of my life. Yes, I actually drew the coveted tag. I love to scout and watch deer so I immediately went to our newly rebuilt cabin in Montana to begin getting acquainted with some big bucks. After a week or so there I returned home to await the opening day. Anxious to get underway on this hunt of a lifetime, I returned to the cabin several days before the opener just to check things out you know. A guy can't do too much scouting when you've got a prize tag in your pocket.

Joanne was with me at the cabin, as she usually is, but this time, we were joined by our good friend, Larry Irwin. Larry lives in western Montana and we'd met in the forest a couple of years earlier, through some mutual friends. We discovered that we had a lot in common, mainly hunting, and have become good friends since. I talked Larry into joining SCI and since, he and his wife, Mary, have met Joanne and I at the SCI convention several times, as well as other places. Larry was now camped in our yard as is quite common during hunting season , as well as about any other time we are there.

Anyway, the opening morning found Larry and I out in the mountains; him after elk while I started my search for a mule buck. I wouldn't turn down a nice bull, but the ridge I was on was some of my favorite deer country and I was able to pass up two real nice 4x4's right at dawn. What a sight they were sky-lined against the pink early morning sky!

They were nice bucks, but not quite nice enough. I was looking for one a year or two older. I continued to pass up bucks until November 1st when Larry and I decided to try a different area and I'd be looking for elk as this primarily was elk country. It was very cold, only 4 degrees above when we left the truck that morning. After a couple hours of sneaking through the squeaky snow, I met up with Larry and after a few minutes of information exchange we went our separate ways. About ten minutes later I killed a 6x5 bull, so that occupied most of the rest of the day.

The next day found me out deer hunting again, but I could now concentrate on deer only because I'd filled my elk tag. I was enjoying the best hunt of my life, and that's saying quite a lot, as I've done much hunting including, as you now know, Africa, Alaska and Canada. I continued to look for just the right buck and once when I came back to the cabin in the middle of the day (something I very seldom do) to take Joanne for a short ride around the mountain, we were fortunate enough to see two real nice 4x4 bucks. She could not understand why I did not shoot one of them, but they were just not quite old enough or wide enough. I was very confident that the upcoming rut would prove interesting, indeed. I usually figure the rut in this area to last from about November 10th to 15th.

Then in the very late afternoon of November 8th I watched a very large buck come down off the ridge and barrel through the small bunch of deer I had been watching. The entire herd just leaped over each other to try to get out of his way. Bucks and does both! That big buck was king and he knew it as well as they did. I knew it too. It sure didn't go unnoticed from my vantage point. Too late to go after him, too far to shoot and way too big to forget about! When I got back to the cabin that night I told Larry about him. I told him I'd found the one I wanted. The next morning I had him drop me off way before daylight as he went on to go elk hunting. I walked a ways out that ridge before first light and hunkered down in the weeds and the wind. Remember that this country all burned a couple of years ago, so there's not much to hide behind.

As it started to get light enough to see good, I noticed several does and small bucks coming up out of the bottom of the draw I was watching and feeding towards me, but going somewhat off to my right. They eventually bedded down after feeding and milling around there on that open hillside. Soon a bigger 4x4 buck came up out of the same canyon and made things uneasy for the resting does as well as the smaller bucks. I had no sensible choice but to lay low and be patient. Due to the nearness of the rut, I knew it was just a matter of time 'til the "king" buck would return to check the ten to twelve does I was patiently watching. I was resting my head on a small partially burned log about six inches in diameter. My left-handed, model 700 Remington in 7mm magnum caliber lay beside me with the scope covers off and the magnification turned to 4 power. My 10x42 Leica binocular was in constant use and seldom left my eyes, when they did, it was very slowly. The shooting sticks I always carry lay close enough to easily reach in case I needed them. I had a shell in the barrel and the safety was on. I was ready.

About 9:00 a.m., I saw the old monarch come up out of the little canyon, cross an old skid road and stop to thrash a blue elderberry bush. When he finished that he proceeded up the hill towards me, stopping to roust a young doe out of her bed, then check to see if she was receptive to his intentions. She wasn't! He paused there just long enough for my

Waiting at the cabin for Larry's return.

165 grain bullet to cross the 200 yards that separated us and find his five and one half year old heart. He stood still there a few seconds before falling one last time and then slid backwards down the mountain to come to rest against a black charred stump. I savored the moment. I didn't move for about ten minutes, when I finally ejected the one empty cartridge. The remaining deer had not ran off or seemed too excited because they did not know I was there. They had not seen me, only heard a loud noise and had seen the "king" fall. As I finally got to my feet the remaining deer ambled off. Thus ended the best hunt of my life. The 8+ years of scouting had paid off. When I finally hiked the mile and a half to my Dodge with a very big load and then drove to the cabin I laid the horns and cape on the porch to await Larry's response. I'm sure he was not aware of bucks of that caliber in that area. He is now!

If there ever was a success story in game management, the mule deer plan in western Montana is it. I for one, really appreciate it. I thank Montana for this 29-inch-wide "book" deer. I dearly love hunting and being in Montana and if it wasn't for my appointment to Oregon's Access and Habitat board in December of 2001, I'd probably be a Montana resident now.

A few days later while counting my blessings, I realized that I'd just taken a 6x5 bull elk and a 6x5 mule deer while I was 65 years old. I hope my children and grand kids can have hunting like that. (But I'd sure like just one more Montana mule deer tag)

Joanne, grandson Ryan and the author with Ryan's big Kudu.

Chapter Twenty-six

SAFARI IN NAMIBIA

I mentioned earlier that I'd gotten involved in Safari Club International. After serving two years as president of the Portland Chapter of SCI, I was elected as the regional representative for this region, which at that time included Oregon, Washington, a chapter in northern Idaho and one in southern British Columbia, Canada. This position put me on the board of directors for SCI. Altogether I served six years in that capacity, which meant that as regional rep., I was supposed to attend fundraisers and chapter events in this large area. I got to attend a lot of banquets and fundraisers!

At one of these up in Washington state I bought a safari for two hunters in Namibia for plains game. We had not been to or hunted Namibia, but it was on my mind to possibly go sometime.

Joanne wanted to go along, but did not want to hunt, so I needed a hunting partner. I've always been very cautious in choosing who I hunt with and this was no exception. We decided to take our sixteen-year-old grandson, Ryan Harrel, with us. We couldn't have made a better choice. It was really fun having him along and showing him some of what we'd seen before, but also experiencing a country that was new to us too. This, of course was Ryan's first and undoubtedly our last safari to Africa.

After much corresponding via email, the professional hunter in Namibia (Danie van Ellewee), and I thought we had everything figured out. The hunt was now officially booked and we'd leave on the 6th of June, 2004. We left two days after school was out. Possibly Ryan could have left a few days earlier, but we wanted to be here to see our granddaughter, Niki Fowler, graduate from high school.

We flew from Portland to Atlanta and then direct to Johannesburg, South Africa, then on to Windhoek, the capitol of Namibia. This was

Ryan's first time to fly. During the next few weeks he would experience many more "firsts". We were met at the airport in Windhoek, by our "PH", Danie.

After getting everything loaded into his dual cab Toyota truck we rode about two and a half hours to get to Chaibis ranch, where Danie introduced us to the owners of this 40,000 acre cattle ranch. Butter and his wife, Hanelie, were great hosts. Very remote here, the nearest neighbor is one and a half hours away by car.

The next morning after checking our rifles we were off to the back of the ranch when Danie saw some baboons across a draw and of course Ryan wanted one of those. He took a fairly long shot at a huge old male and MISSED. Well the pressure was off now and I don't think he missed again on that trip. In fact he shot very well, partially due, I'm sure to his dad and I taking him to practice so often. Later in the day they stalked kudu and gemsbuck, but never got a shot.

Day two was different, Ryan got a nice gold-medal springbuck. He had broken the ice now. Very early on the third day Ryan spotted a large kudu bull standing in the early morning shade by himself. Danie came to a sudden stop and the stalk was on. Soon we heard him shoot a couple of times from the other side of a ridge. When they came back to get the Toyota, Ryan was all smiles. Who wouldn't be after just getting a 53" kudu bull?

I had not intended to shoot one of the mountain zebras that inhabit this part of Africa, as I'd passed on shooting the Burchell's zebra before, but this species was different. They were more like hunting sheep; up high in the rocks and very alert and spooky. Later we saw a herd that we were able to close in on and my .375 H&H magnum did the job again, on a very big stallion. Our trackers on that day were very young; only fifteen and sixteen years old, but they were able to butcher that big animal and carried most of it to the truck. The surprising thing was that they were also very small boys, less than 100 pounds each, I'm certain. But they could carry a quarter of that big zebra!

It was about this time that Butter spotted another bunch of baboons and this time Ryan did not miss. He got a big old male. Butter's big Caterpillar tractor had broken down a couple of years before and it had cost him a small fortune in their money to get parts from the USA and have them shipped to Namibia. Even here at home, Cat parts aren't cheap. When he got the parts and went out on the ranch to put the Cat together again, he realized that the baboons had caused him a lot more trouble. They had stolen a stainless steel hydraulic line about 24" long but one that had several twists and turns in it. Not just a straight piece that he could replace! So the Cat was still sitting there, and still broke down. Poor old Butter! He had no love for baboons. He would now have to find a way to order another piece from the USA and hopefully he could find some hunter to deliver it to him.

I was next up to shoot and I ended up with a good springbuck, but I did a very poor job of shooting. Consequently, Danie had to track it a long way and then carry it a long way to the Toyota.

Namibia is known for its gemsbuck and I definitely wanted one. I had missed one in South Africa several years before and now I wanted another chance. I now believe that it is nearly impossible for me to hit a gemsbuck with a rifle. I don't know why, but they just seem to dodge my bullets. I had to miss a couple more here before I was finally able to connect on one. All the game here seemed very flighty, especially the gemsbuck and zebra. It was THE place to go to though for Kudu. I'll bet we saw at least forty mature bulls, 50" and over.

My long-sought-after Gemsbuck bull.

On the last evening of the last day after we'd hunted all day for a gemsbuck for Ryan, he finally got his chance. It wasn't even very far from the truck and it was standing still when he shot. Now he was happy again! Looked kinda down there for awhile as he did want a gemsbuck too!

All in all, we had a very good hunt with Danie and Butter and last winter when Danie visited us here in Oregon, he offered Ryan a season of work with "Into Africa Hunting Adventures". Sounds like Ryan wants to go too.

When we left Namibia, we flew to Johannesburg where we got a hotel room and then the following morning we flew to Zimbabwe to see Victoria Falls for a few days. That is sure a beautiful place, but Ryan didn't like all the pressure the "blacks" put on us to buy their carvings, etc. Got some good pictures of the famous falls and even went out of town a short distance to learn about and ride elephants. Great trip! We did enjoy taking Ryan with us. I'm sure he'll return to hunt there again some day and I've asked him to remember his grandmother and I when he does.

Chapter Twenty-seven

ELK HUNTING WITH CATHY

Oregon has very short elk seasons. The first is only four days long and the second is only seven days long. For the '04 elk season I had drawn a special muzzleloader tag in eastern Oregon, which I failed to fill, so I was not able to hunt near our home as I quite often do.

Our oldest daughter, Cathy, had not hunted for several years, but this year she decided she wanted to hunt elk near our homes. She tried it on her own for a couple days and then I told her I'd like to take her for a walk the next day. She arranged to get the day off from her job and I told her we'd go for a walk, probably wouldn't see anything, but we'd get out anyway.

She carried her little 6.5 Remington and a binocular while I carried my binocular and the shooting sticks that I almost always have when I'm hunting. I did not carry a rifle, although it would have been legal to do so, I wasn't going to be tempted to shoot a bull for her. No way! My kids have always shot their own game. We parked my Dodge right at daylight and started hiking into an area that sometimes holds elk. All I was hoping for was one little old spike for her to have a chance at. There was some elk sign, but nothing to write home about, although it was a great day to be out. This was all new country to her and I was enjoying showing it to her. We made a large circuitous hike, stopping about 10:30 for lunch. After lunch we proceeded to finish the circle and arrived at the pickup about 1:30. Both being a little tired, we chose to head home for a quick nap and then go out again in the late afternoon.

She arrived back at my house about 3:30 and we decided to try a different place for our short evening hunt. By the time we drove there, parked, walked in and got ourselves situated we only had an hour or so to hunt, but sometimes that is the best hour.

We sat down on a little low ridge about thirty to forty feet apart and facing different directions.

After about ten minutes I thought I heard something, but my hearing is so bad that I relied on Cathy to let me know if she heard anything. Only a few seconds later, I thought I heard it again and when I looked over at her, I knew immediately that she too had heard it. It sounded to me rather like someone was cutting a trail over across the canyon from us. I could hear the frequent hacking, but couldn't understand why anyone would be cutting trail in that particular area. We hurriedly agreed to move up the ridge to get somewhat closer. As soon as I stood up, turned around and took a few steps, I knew it was antlers clashing that we were hearing. It was right in the middle of the blacktail deer rut, so it wasn't too surprising. Nevertheless, I wanted to get to where I could see the fight. We ran about 50 yards and while I was waiting for Cathy, I glassed across the little canyon and could see the back half of an elk showing behind a tree. I immediately thought it looked too light to be anything except a bull, but I still wanted to see those bucks fighting too, so I kept looking around. Suddenly, about the time Cathy got up by me, the elk moved ahead and was completely hidden behind the small tree, but she had seen it too. Almost instantly it shot back out from behind the tree, backwards. It was fighting with another bull and the opponent had just shoved it out in plain sight of us, but before we knew it, or could react, the one we could see had shoved the other one backwards until we could see neither of them. This was NOT a sparring match as I've seen many times. These two big bulls were fighting for all they were worth, but this was late November (in fact, the day before Thanksgiving) and the elk rut should have been over long ago. Why they were fighting so hard at this time of year, I have no idea, but they were. We watched it go on for several minutes, all the time Cathy was trying to get a good rest and a good bead on the one that we most often saw. (the other was behind more brush) As soon as the shoving slowed a little, so that the one big bull was stationary for more than two seconds, I told her to shoot. At the sound of the shot the bull turned and ran to our right and out of our sight. Meanwhile we got glimpses of the opponent. Then, surprise, the one she'd shot at came back and she got another couple of shots, with at least one of those missing the bull. The huge bull was immediately lost in the reprod in that area and quite honestly, showed no visible sign of being hit, but you have to go look. We had two choices: go the long way around the head of the canyon she shot over or cross the brush-infested canyon right here where we were. That was my choice, as I wanted to go as directly to the place where the bull had stood as I could. Cathy followed me across and it was almost dark when we started looking for blood. We had no problem whatsoever finding the site where the fight took place. Man was it ever torn up! Looked like someone had been there with a rototiller! While I stood there in awe at the site, Cathy found the blood trail, so we took off on it. Now I was beginning to wish that I had brought my old 7mm Remington along. Cathy had a hard time keeping right up with me and I didn't want her out of my reach in case we found the bull still alive. We had failed to take a flashlight with us when we left the Dodge, so it was not easy trying to identify blood on the ferns and logs in the growing darkness. We went as far as we could, which wasn't really very far (about 150 yards) when we had to quit the trail. I tied a long red ribbon there on one of the many eight- to ten-foot tall Douglas fir trees and we headed for home. We both knew where we'd spend Thanksgiving morning.

We managed to find our way through the thick reprod to our pickup without a flashlight, and came home hopeful about Thanksgiving morning and finding the bull. We were joined the next morning by son-in-laws, Bill and Jim, along with grandson, Ryan Harrel, as well as son Dan and another neighbor. We had lots of help and hoped to find the bull either dead or still alive. After placing a couple guys in strategic locations to watch the rest of us proceeded to the ribbon I'd hung the night before, where we were going to spread out and all go in different locations to look for blood. During the night we had experienced the first good hard rain of the season, so our hopes of finding blood were slimmer than they had been the night before. We needed that rain like Custer needed another Indian. I had showed them the area where the two bulls fought and also where we had trailed him, now it was time to get to work. Or maybe I should say "get lucky"! We split up there at the ribbon and I had only gone about 30 feet in that thick reprod when I heard Cathy shoot right close to me, although I could not see her (nor anyone else). She fired two quick shots and then answered our shouts. She had seen the bull's horns across a little brushy ravine and knew that he was still standing up because she'd seen also seen part of his hind quarters moving behind the thick fir trees. The two shots put him down and we were all so glad and felt so lucky to have it work out that way. At this time we could only see bits and pieces of his tan hide through the brush and we find a decent way to get over to him. When we got there, SURPRISE, SURPRISE! It was a different bull entirely. A raghorn with an odd shaped horn! Talk about a disappointment! Who would have ever thought that there would be another bull there after we had been so noisy in our approach? We weren't real quiet because we thought the bull would either be dead or badly wounded. We did not expect him or any other to be that close to where we'd quit the night before. Our spirits were not the highest now. Due to the holiday plans we were expected back home around noon. We made that alright, but we had to hurry to butcher, pack and get the meat hung up.

I spent the next morning and several more days in that area trying to find the big one she hit, but to no avail. I did find his tracks and was able to follow them about one-third of a mile but then lost them in some reprod that was too thick to even stand up in. I sure hope he survived, we want another crack at him this year. Meanwhile, Cathy is shopping for a bigger rifle.

Now that season is behind me (like so many others) but Joanne and I are planning and looking forward to a trip to New Zealand in the near future where we hope to hunt red stag and tahr. You've got to have something to look forward to and when the good Lord calls me home I only hope I don't have a hunting trip planned or any unused tags in my pocket.

THE END

LISTING OF BOOKS

Additional copies of **THE TRAIL OF A SPORTSMAN** *and many other of Stoneydale Press' books on outdoor recreation, big game hunting, or historical reminisces centered around the Northern Rocky Mountain region, are available at many book stores and sporting goods stores, or direct from Stoneydale Press. If you'd like more information, you can contact us by calling a Toll Free Number,* **1-800-735-7006,** *by writing the address at the bottom of the page, or contacting us on the Web at www.stoneydale.com. Here's a partial listing of some of the books that are available including those by the late, revered storyteller Howard Copenhaver.*

Books By Howard Copenhaver

Copenhaver Country, By Howard Copenhaver, *the latest collection of humorous stories. Contains rich humor and studied observations of a land Howard loves and the people he met along the way in a lifetime spent in the wilds. 160 pages, many photographs.*

They Left Their Tracks, By Howard Copenhaver, *Recollections of Sixty Years as a Wilderness Outfitter, 192 pages, clothbound or softcover editions (One of our all-time most popular books.)*

More Tracks, By Howard Copenhaver, *78 Years of Mountains, People & Happiness, 180 pages, clothbound or softcover editions.*

Mule Tracks: The Last of The Story, By Howard Copenhaver. *As one of Montana's most revered storytellers and honored outfitters, Howard spent years leading his mule packstrings through the Bob Marshall Wilderness. Read here of his adventures, misadventures and other wild tales of mules in the wild country. 176 pages, hardcover and softcover editions.*

Historical Reminisces

Indian Trails & Grizzly Tales, By Bud Cheff Sr. *A wonderful collection of stories taken from a lifetime outfitting in Montana's Bob Marshall and Mission Mountain Wilderness areas, by a master woodsman. 232 pages, available in clothbound and softcover editions.*

70,000 Miles Horseback In The Wilds of Idaho, By Don Habel. *Don Habel worked as an outfitter in the Idaho wilderness for more than forty years and has put together a wonderfully detailed and sensitive, as well as occasionally humorous, reminisce of his adventures in the wilds. 180 pages, softcover.*

The Potts' Factor Versus Murphy's Law, By Stan Potts. *Life story of famous Idaho outfitter Stan Potts, lots of photographs. 192 pages.*

Mules & Mountains, By Margie E. Hahn, *the story of Walt Hahn, Forest Service Packer, 164 pages, clothbound or softcover editions.*

Dreams Across The Divide: Stories of the Montana Pioneers, Edited by Linda Wostrel, Foreword by Stephen Ambrose. *Stories and photos of the first pioneers to settle in Montana. 448 pages.*

The Packer's Field Manual, *By Bob Hoverson. Featuring use of the Decker Pack Saddle, this manual written by one of the top experts in the country will literally provide you with every detail necessary to successfully pack with the Decker Pack Saddle. 6x9-inch softcover format, 192 pages, many photographs and illustrations by Roger Inghram.*

Hunting Chukar, *By Richard O'Toole. This authoritative and detailed guide to hunting the West's most elusive game bird, the chukar, provides both experience and knowledge taken from 35-plus years of experience. Chapters on locating birds, tactics used in hunting them, gear, the choice and use of dogs, and many photographs. 6x9-inch format, softcover, 12 chapters and an appendix.*

Solving Elk Hunting Problems, *By Mike Lapinski. Subtitled "Simple Solutions to The Elk Hunting Riddle," this book, in 15 chapters and more than 80 photographs tells you now to cope with specific problems you'll encounter in the field – a hung-up bull, changes in elk behavior under heavy hunting pressure, peak rut activity, and so on. 6x9-inch format, both softcover and hardcover editions.*

High Pressure Elk Hunting, *By Mike Lapinski. The latest book available on hunting elk that have become educated to the presence of more hunters working them. Lots of info on hunting these elk.192 pages, many photographs, hardcover or softcover.*

Bugling for Elk, *By Dwight Schuh, the bible on hunting early-season elk. A recognized classic, 164 pages, softcover edition only.*

A Hunt For the Great Northern, *By Herb Neils. This acclaimed new novel utilizes the drama of a hunting camp as the setting for a novel of intrigue, mystery, adventure and great challenge set in the woods of northwestern Montana. 204 pages, softcover.*

Ghost of The Wilderness, *By James "Mac" Mackee. A dramatic story of the pursuit of the mountain lion, the Ghost of The Wilderness. A tremendous tale of what Jim MacKee went through over several seasons in his quest for a trophy mountain lion in the wilds of Montana. 160 pages, softcover.*

The Woodsman And His Hatchet, *By Bud Cheff. Subtitled "Eighty Years on Wilderness Survival," this book gives you practical, common sense advice on survival under emergency conditions in the wilderness. 5½x8½-inch, softcover format.*

Memoirs of An Idaho Elk Hunter, *By Jens Andersen. This big book captures the vitality and romance of a lifetime spent hunting elk in Idaho and Montana. A superb read, many color photographs and illustrations. 216 pages, hardcover only.*

Coyote Hunting, *By Phil Simonski. Presents basics on hunting coyotes as well as caring for the pelts, 126 pages, many photographs, softcover only.*

Elk Hunting in the Northern Rockies, *By Ed Wolff. Uses expertise of five recognized elk hunting experts to show the five basic concepts used to hunt elk. Another of our very popular books, 162 pages, many photographs.*

So You Really Want To Be a Guide, By Dan Cherry. *The latest and single most authoritative source on what it takes to be a guide today. This book is an excellent guideline to a successful guiding career. Softcover edition only.*

Hunting Open Country Mule Deer, By Dwight Schuh. *Simply the best and most detailed book ever done for getting in close to big mule deer. The ultimate mule deer book by a recognized master, 14 chapters, 180 pages.*

Montana Hunting Guide, By Dale A. Burk, *the most comprehensive and fact-filled guidebook available on hunting in Montana, 192 pages, clothbound or softcover editions.*

Taking Big Bucks, By Ed Wolff. *Subtitled "Solving the Whitetail Riddle," this book presents advice from top whitetail experts with an emphasis on hunting western whitetails. 176 pages, 62 photographs.*

Radical Elk Hunting Strategies, By Mike Lapinski. *Takes over where other books on early-season elk hunting leave off to give advice on what the hunter must do to adapt to changing conditions. 162 pages, 70 photographs.*

Western Hunting Guide, By Mike Lapinski, *the most thorough guide on hunting the western states available. A listing of where-to-go in the western states alone makes the book a valuable reference tool. 168 pages, softcover.*

Quest for Giant Bighorns, By Duncan Gilchrist. *Comprehensive overview on hunting bighorn sheep everywhere they're hunted; detailed how-to, where-to with lots of photos. 224 pages, softcover.*

Quest for Dall Rams, By Duncan Gilchrist. *The best source book ever put together on the beautiful Dall sheep, it's crammed with solid how-to and where-to information on hunting Dall sheep. 224 pages, 88 photographs, many charts, softcover format.*

Montana–Land of Giant Rams, Vol. III, By Duncan Gilchrist. *The best source and most acclaimed book available on hunting bighorn sheep in Montana. Updated and expanded from his earlier volumes on the same subject. 224 pages, many photographs, softcover format.*

Successful Big Game Hunting, By Duncan Gilchrist. *For more than four decades now, Duncan Gilchrist has hunted across North America as well as in Africa and New Zealand. This book touches every aspect of what it takes to be a successful hunter. 176 pages, 82 photographs, both softcover and hardcover formats.*

Field Care Handbook, By Duncan Gilchrist and Bill Sager. *The most comprehensive field guide available for the care of big game, birds, fish and other species. Illustrated by many of Duncan's photographs taken in the field. 168 pages, many photographs and illustrations, comb binding so it will lay flat while you use it.*

Cookbooks

Camp Cookbook, Featuring Recipes for Fixing Both at Home and in Camp, With Field Stories by Dale A. Burk, *216 pages, comb binding.*

That Perfect Batch: The Hows and Whys of Making Sausage and Jerky, By Clem Stechelin. *Detailed instruction on techniques of making sausage and jerky at home from wild game, beef, etc. 116 pages, many photographs, comb binding.*

Cooking for Your Hunter, By Miriam Jones. *A thorough cookbook of recipes using wild game, plus others for a variety of foods. Miriam helps you understand how cooking with wild game is simply a part of normal cooking. 180 pages, comb binding.*

Cooking on Location, By Cheri Eby. *Exhaustive content for cooking on location in the outdoors, from menu planning to camp organization, meal preparation, and recipes for all sorts and styles of dishes. 139 pages, color photos and illustrations, comb binding.*

Venison As You Like It, By Ned Dobson. *A manual on getting the most from game meat, with over 200 recipes and instructions on using a variety of cooking methods. Detailed index, softcover.*

STONEYDALE PRESS PUBLISHING COMPANY

523 Main Street • Box 188
Stevensville, Montana 59870
Phone: 406-777-2729
Website: www.stoneydale.com